Pine Needle Basketry

From Forest Floor
to Finished Project

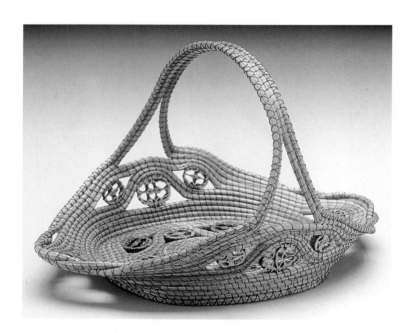

JUDY MOFIELD MALLOW

LARK
CRAFTS

An Imprint of Sterling Publishing Co., Inc.
New York

WWW.LARKCRAFTS.COM

Editor: Chris Rich
Photography: Evan Bracken
Art Direction: Kathy Holmes
Production: Elaine Thompson
Illustration: Kay Stafford

The Library of Congress has cataloged the hardcover edition as follows:
Mallow, Judy Mofield, 1949–
    Pine needle basketry : from forest floor to finished project / by Judy
Mofield Mallow.
      p.   cm.
    Includes index.
    ISBN 1-887374-14-0
    1. Basket making.   2. Pine needle crafts.   I. Title.
TT879.B3M35   1997
746.41'2--dc20   96-26504

10 9 8 7 6 5 4 3

Published by Lark Crafts, An Imprint of
Sterling Publishing Co., Inc.
387 Park Avenue South, New York, N.Y. 10016

First Paperback Edition 2010
© 2001 by Judy Mofield Mallow

Distributed in Canada by Sterling Publishing,
c/o Canadian Manda Group, 165 Dufferin Street
Toronto, Ontario, Canada M6K 3H6

Distributed in the United Kingdom by GMC Distribution Services,
Castle Place, 166 High Street, Lewes, East Sussex, England BN7 1XU

Distributed in Australia by Capricorn Link (Australia) Pty Ltd.
P.O. Box 704, Windsor, NSW 2756 Australia

If you have questions or comments about this book, please contact:
Lark Crafts
67 Broadway, Asheville, NC 28801
(828) 253-0467

Manufactured in China

ISBN 13: 978-1-887374-14-9 (hardcover) 978-1-60059-603-2 (paperback)

For information about custom editions, special sales, premium and corporate purchases, please contact Sterling
Special Sales Department at 800-805-5489 or specialsales@sterlingpub.com.

For information about desk and examination copies available to college and university professors, requests must
be submitted to academic@larkbooks.com. Our complete policy can be found at www.larkcrafts.com.

Contents

INTRODUCTION

Pine needle basketry offers both the beginning basketmaker and the expert an equal opportunity for satisfaction. Even if you've never seen a forest carpeted with fragrant pine needle clusters, let alone created a basket from natural materials, you'll quickly discover that you don't need the patience of Job or the hands of a surgeon to make a basket worth boasting about. In fact, with the help of the instructions in this book, you'll construct your first basket in a single day. Highly skilled basketmakers who have longed to try new materials will find that pine needles offer an entirely new aesthetic.

Making coiled pine needle projects is downright easy. Imagine coiling a thick length of rope around and around itself on a flat surface while you stitch the coils to each other to hold them together. You'd end up with something that looked like a round place mat. Now picture yourself holding a small bundle of pine needles while you coil and stitch them in the same fashion. What would you get? The flat, round bottom of a pine needle basket. Pine needles aren't very long, of course, so when you make a basket, you feed new needles into the coil as you stitch. What about shaping the walls of the basket? Easy. When the basket bottom is as large as you'd like, you stitch the succeeding coils on top of each other.

Endless variations are possible: in shapes, in stitches and thread, in the centers you use, in the colors of your needles (pine needles are easy to dye), and in the embellishments you add. Tall, elegant baskets made with nothing but undyed needles and brown thread; perfectly rounded sewing baskets; trays with handles—these and hundreds of other projects are all within reach once you've mastered the basic technique.

To get the most from this book, start with the first chapter, "Materials and Tools." Once you're sure you have everything you need, follow the step-by-step instructions in chapter 2 to make your first basket. By doing so, you'll learn all the basics and prepare yourself for more challenging work. Then browse through chapters 3 and 4. In them, you'll find instructions for adding the elements that make pine needle projects so different from one another. Don't bother to study these two chapters as if they were textbook material. Instead, select a project (you'll find more than 40 in chapter 5) and refer to the chart that comes with it. This project-specific chart will let you know which sections of chapters 3 and 4 to read closely.

In the remaining chapters, you'll find a bit of history and photos of some of the finest pine needle work in existence. Try not to let envy consume you when you see these stunning pieces! If you bring along your patience, take the time to practice, and let your imagination act as your guide, you'll soon be transforming pine needles into projects just as lovely.

CHAPTER ONE

MATERIALS AND TOOLS

IF YOU'RE DREADING the thought of depleting your bank account to finance another hobby, you can stop worrying right now. Most of the required tools for this craft probably reside in your kitchen cabinets or sewing basket already, and the few that don't are very inexpensive to make or buy.

Pine needles are often free for the gathering, depending, of course, on where you live. If you're fortunate, you'll have a few pine trees on your property or a pine forest nearby.

PINE NEEDLES

Pine needles are actually leaves and usually grow in clusters of two or three. As you can see in the photo below, a cap (or sheath) binds the heads of the needles in each cluster. For most projects, you'll remove these caps; to embellish others, you'll leave them on.

GATHERING NEEDLES

Dried, brown needles may be gathered whenever you like, but the best time is just after the clusters fall from the trees, as cool weather begins to set in. Pick up the clusters one by one, straight from the ground, avoiding those buried by others, as buried needles may be mildewed or infested with insects. Group the clusters into small bundles, with their caps facing in one direction, and secure each bundle with a rubber band. Leave broken needles where they can continue to provide valuable mulch for the trees around them.

You may also collect green needles and dry them yourself by spreading them out on screens or newspapers in full sunlight for two to three weeks, turning them occasionally to make sure that they color evenly.

For dyed-needle projects in light colors, needles that have been dried in sunlight won't do, as they'll be too dark to allow the dye to show properly. Instead, collect green needles and dry them in the dark until they've faded from brilliant to light green.

When collecting green needles, pluck only what you need. Stripping or killing a tree for its needles is like killing an elephant for its ivory—destructive and unnecessary.

Never use fresh green needles, as the coils in a basket made with them will shrink as the needles dry, leaving you with coils that are loose at best and a basket that is downright floppy at worst.

Once the green needles are exposed to light, they'll eventually turn brown anyway.

STORING NEEDLES

Before storing bundles of dried needles (brown or light green), you must rid them of the few insect varieties that don't find pine needle rosin distasteful by placing them in the freezer for a few days. Then place them in cardboard boxes. If the boxes are kept in a cool, dry environment, the needles will last for years. (Don't bother to freeze the needles if you'll be using them to make a basket right away; they'll be soaked in hot water to sterilize and soften them just before you use them.)

COUNTING NEEDLES—DON'T!

Counting out pine needles for each project—even if there were a truly accurate way to determine how many you need—would turn this entertaining craft into a nightmare, so don't even try! You'll have a better sense of how to gauge quantities once you've made your first few baskets of different sizes. Take a look at the chart that follows. As a rule of thumb, a 16-ounce (454 g) bundle of needles will make one large basket.

Bundle Weight		Bundle Circumference	
Ounces	Grams	Inches	Centimeters
4	113	5	12.7
8	227	6-1/2	16.5
16	454	9	22.9

TOWEL

To prepare your pine needles, you'll soak them in hot water, drain them, and wrap them in an old bath towel to keep them moist, soft, and pliable as you work.

CONTAINER FOR SOAKING NEEDLES

Any waterproof container that's long enough not to bend the needles will do. Old baking pans and plastic wallpaper containers work well.

SEWING NEEDLES

Your sewing needles must be sharp enough to pierce the pine needle coils without tearing the needles and must have eyes large enough to accommodate the thread you've selected. Cotton darners and chenille or embroidery needles are good choices. Curved and/or short needles come in handy when you're stitching tight shapes such as the narrow necks of bottle- or jug-shaped projects, so keep an assortment on hand.

SCISSORS

Purchase a small pair of scissors with sharp, pointed blades. Embroidery scissors or small craft scissors are ideal.

MASKING TAPE

You'll use tape to mark what's known as the "starting point" on your basket, where you take your very first stitch. This point serves as a reference for adding new stitches, for locating handles, for shifting the coil placement during the shaping of a basket, and for ending the coil that forms your basket, so keeping track of it is critical. Masking tape also comes in handy when you want to ensure accurate and symmetrical placement of decorative embellishments.

CLOTHESPINS AND RUBBER BANDS

Spring-loaded clothespins are handy for holding thread taut and coils in place during different stages of the coiling process. For binding together bundles of gathered pine needles, use rubber bands.

THREAD

Almost any kind of thread that will fit through the eye of a large sewing needle will work. I use nylon upholstery thread on most of my projects because it lasts longer than many other materials, but project longevity may not be as high a priority for you. Following is a list of some of the more popular threads:

~ Nylon upholstery thread will last for many years. It comes in a wide variety of colors, including earth tones, and is available from upholstery shops and many craft-supply stores.

~ Raffia is a natural material made from the leaf stalks of the raffia palm. Once used only in Africa, where it was incorporated into baskets, mats, bags, and clothes, it is now commonly available at craft-supply stores. Purchase either the treated or untreated variety.

To prepare untreated raffia for use in pine needle projects, cut off the knot that holds the raffia strips together and soak the bundle in warm water for several minutes. Straighten the fibers by hand and allow them to hang-dry. Split to the desired width and flatten by running your thumb and one finger along each length.

Thread natural raffia so that the thick end is at the eye of your sewing needle, as this is the end most likely to shred.

~ Synthetic raffia is available at many craft-supply stores in bright, lasting colors. It doesn't shred as easily as natural raffia and is even in texture, so it's somewhat easier to work with. In addition, because synthetic raffia is sold in balls or skeins, you won't waste quite as much as you might when working with shorter lengths of natural raffia.

~ Artificial sinew looks similar to raffia and also comes in bright colors. It's exceptionally strong, however, and can be split to make a thin thread for use in miniature baskets.

~ Waxed linen comes in many brilliant colors. This strong, durable thread can be purchased at craft-supply stores.

~ Polyester thread, monofilament (fishing line), non-stretching yarns, carpet thread, and four-ply candlewick thread will all work well.

WIRE (OPTIONAL)

When it's inserted into the center of the pine needle coil, wire serves to reinforce some types of basket handles and large basket rims. Depending upon the size of the part to be reinforced, use 16- to 24-gauge wire. Some crafters also use fine-gauge wire as a substitute for thread.

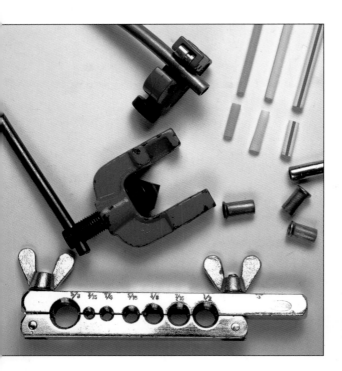

GAUGE

To make the continuous coil from which most pine needle projects are formed, you'll keep feeding new pine needles into the coil as you stitch it in place. A gauge—a short, narrow length of plastic or metal tubing that fits around the loose needles—will hold the needles as you work and will also help keep your coil consistent in thickness.

When you add needles to the coil (usually after every two or three stitches), you'll slip them into the center of those already in the gauge, adding as many as it takes to keep the gauge's grip on the needles secure but not too tight.

Gauge diameters can vary, depending on how thick you want your coils to be, but 3/8" (1 cm) gauges are the most common. To make gauges, just cut 1" (2.5 cm) lengths of plastic, copper,

or aluminum tubing. The metal bands from pencil erasers also work, as do short lengths of soda straw.

I use a flanging tool (available at hardware stores) to flare one end of each metal gauge because a flared end makes it easier to separate the needles within when I need to insert new needles. When you're working on miniature baskets, no gauge is necessary.

NEEDLE-NOSE PLIERS

When your fingers aren't strong enough to pull the sewing needle through a thick pine needle coil, use these pliers instead.

ROTARY TOOL OR ELECTRIC DRILL (OPTIONAL)

While neither of these tools is essential, either will prove helpful when you want to add leather, wood, or gourd centers, or embellishments. A rotary tool is simply a mini-drill, bits for which come in many different sizes and shapes. You'll need a 1/16" (1.5 mm) bit no matter which type of drilling tool you use.

SHELLAC, PAINTBRUSH, AND AMMONIA (OPTIONAL)

Covering your finished project with shellac isn't absolutely necessary, but it will help to stiffen and preserve the coils. Before starting, always test the shellac on a piece of scrap wood or on the bottom of your basket. If the shellac doesn't dry by the following morning, it has probably gone bad and should be discarded. One tip: Don't throw away a basket that you've accidentally coated with bad shellac. Just apply a coat of new shellac over the old.

Brush on the shellac with a 1-1/2" or 2" (3.8 or 5.1 cm) paintbrush and allow the coat to dry thoroughly. On large baskets and trays, a second coat will help to stiffen the work further for additional support. (Spray shellac or clear acrylic spray may be substituted on smaller projects.) To clean your paintbrush, rinse it in household ammonia.

PARAFFIN AND BEESWAX (OPTIONAL)

A coat of melted paraffin and beeswax provides a protective, gloss-free alternative to a coat of shellac and won't discolor threads or dyed pine needles. Because beeswax can be costly, however, I use this mixture only to coat special, dyed pine-needle baskets.

To wax a basket, first ban children and pets from your working area! Next, preheat your oven to 150°F to 200°F (66°C to 93°C) and line a shallow baking pan with aluminum foil. Then carefully melt a combination of one part paraffin and two parts beeswax over low heat in a double boiler. Watch your step; these substances can cause bad burns. If the mixture begins to smoke, remove it from the heat until it cools a bit; never allow it to boil over or burn. (If you don't own a double boiler, set a metal colander in a large pan of water and prop an empty can in the colander.)

Using a sponge brush, dab the melted mixture all over your basket. Don't be shocked when your work of art becomes something less than gorgeous—it will! As soon as you've finished, place the incredibly ugly, wax-coated basket in the foil-lined pan and put the pan in the oven.

Watch closely; never leave a waxed basket unattended in a hot oven. Within five to ten minutes, the wax will have been absorbed into the basket coils. Make sure that no unmelted wax remains. Then remove the basket from the oven and place it on a piece of waxed paper or aluminum foil to dry and harden.

Lint-Free Cloth

Rubbing a shellac- or wax-coated basket vigorously with this cloth will remove any loose pine needle ends.

Plastic or Wire Rings (Optional)

These rings, several sizes of which are sold at craft-supply stores, are used to make woven teneriffe designs (see pages 39-44).

Fabric Dyes (Optional)

Ordinary fabric dyes, available from grocery and craft-supply stores, can add color to any pine needle project. For information on dyeing needles, turn to pages 24–25.

Chapter Two

Making Your First Basket

Almost every pine needle creation, whether it's a basket, tray, or abstract sculpture, is made using the same simple technique—stitching a continuous coil of pine needles to itself. Once you've finished the basket described in this chapter, you'll have learned how to

~ make a thread-wrapped coil center

~ stitch the coil together with a plain stitch

~ add pine needles and thread

~ shape the sides of the basket

~ taper the coil to finish it off

~ backstitch along to the rim to reinforce it

In fact, you'll have all the skills you need to make hundreds of attractive pine needle projects.

A list of required tools and materials is provided on this page, but keep in mind that a basket is made up of more than pine needles and thread. A basket reflects its maker. Your mood and your work habits are intangibles that can help make your basket a work of art or turn it into an exercise in frustration.

Many pine needle crafters are perfectionists, so you won't be alone if you're one too, but perfectionism can work for or against you. Being careful will reward you with a finely constructed project. Unrealistically high expectations, however, can turn into a stiff neck, clamped jaws, and a basket that reflects your own tension. When your need to make perfect baskets rages out of control, take a break. Do something else for a while (perfectly, if you must), and try to relax those anxious muscles.

Maybe you're short on patience—one of those folks who's filled with fire for fifteen minutes at a stretch. No problem. Pine needle baskets aren't made under deadlines. Forcing yourself to work with pine needles when you'd rather be hiking under the trees themselves will only leave you with a basket that looks as wild as you feel. Just set your work aside until you really want to pick it up again. And remember that the passionate approach, even if it only lasts for a few minutes at a time—often gives rise to wonderfully imaginative basketry shapes.

One other tip: Many expert pine needle crafters claim that "mistakes" can give birth to imaginative new shapes and stitches. Try leaving just one mistake right where it is; you may be surprised by what it adds to your finished piece.

❦ *Preventing Tangled Threads*

Spooled threads such as nylon and waxed linen have a tendency to curl and then to tangle when you use them. To straighten out a length of thread before you use it, stretch it by standing on one end and pulling on the other.

Materials and Tools

Pine needles

Container for soaking needles

Towel

Sewing needle

Thread

Spring-loaded clothespin

Needle-nose pliers

Scissors

Gauge

Masking tape

Waxed paper or newspaper (optional)

Shellac and paintbrush—or spray acrylic (optional)

Lint-free cloth

❦ *An Apology to "Lefties"*

The instructions in this book were written for right-handed people. If you're left-handed, reverse the hand directions. Hold your basket so that the loose pine needles protrude from the top right. Insert the sewing needle to the left of each stitch and pull it out to the right.

Preparing the Needles

1. Place the pine needles in a container and pour boiling water over them, submerging them from cap to end. Allow the needles to soak for 30 minutes and then drain them well.

2. Remove the caps from the clusters by pulling them off with your fingers or scraping them off with the dull edge of a knife or the outer edge of a scissors blade. (Pull the blade up the sheath towards the caps.) Most of the needles will remain in clusters even with their caps removed, but save any needles that separate from their partners. Although clusters are stronger and will fill your gauge faster, you can use individual needles during the early stages of making your basket or whenever you need to add only one or two needles to your coil.

3. Wrap the de-capped needles in the towel to keep them soft and flexible as you work.

Making the Thread-Wrapped Center

4. Cut a length of thread about 1-1/2 yards (1.4 m) long. Using the knot shown in Figure 1, tie three de-capped clusters together tightly just below the area that was covered by the

---

🌿 Taking Breaks

Towel-wrapped, soaked pine needles will remain workable for several days. If you need to set aside your project for a week or more, either put the damp needles in a plastic bag and place the bag in the freezer, or re-soak the needles for a few minutes before resuming. Don't let them soak too long, as a basket made with waterlogged needles will shrink after your project is stitched together, and the project coils will be loose.

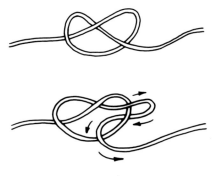

Figure 1

15

caps. Then trim away the short end of the thread and the de-capped needle ends above the knot (see Figure 2).

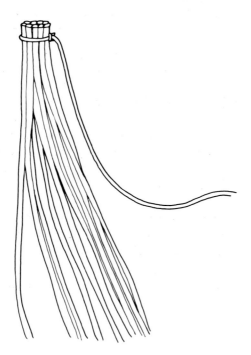

Figure 2

5. Now you'll wrap thread around a 2-1/2" (6.4 cm) section of the tied bundle (see Figure 3). Hold the bundle upright in your left hand, with the thread at the top. Holding the thread in your right hand, twist the needles with your left thumb and forefinger while letting the thread slip through the fingers of your right hand.

6. Push the spiraled thread back towards the knot to form an even, solid covering around the needles. As you do this, use the fingers of your left hand to keep the thread from unwrapping.

7. Repeat Steps 5 and 6 until you've wrapped a 2-1/2" (6.4 cm) section of the bundle. Then hold the wrap in place with a clothespin as you thread the remaining length of thread into a sewing needle. To prevent the wrap from unraveling, insert the sewing needle through it as shown in Figure 3 and pull the thread taut. If your fingers aren't strong enough, use needle-nose pliers to pull the needle through the coil.

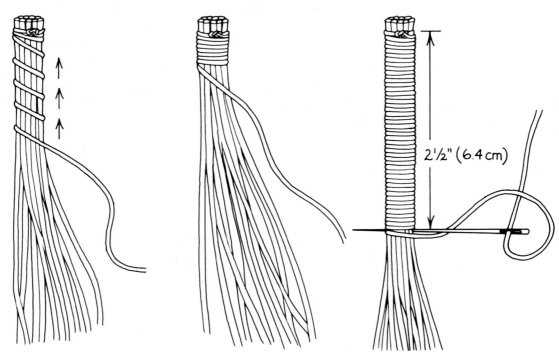

2½" (6.4 cm)

Figure 3

8. To make the wrapped section more flexible, work it a bit by bending it, a little at a time. Then fold it into thirds to form a small oval (see Figure 4). The thread should now emerge from the front surface, and the loose pine needles should be to your left. (In fact, the loose pine needles should always face to the left as you work.)

❦ Shaping Your Basket

The shape of your basket depends in part on the shape of its center. To make an oval tray, for example, you'd fold the initial coil to form an elongated oval.

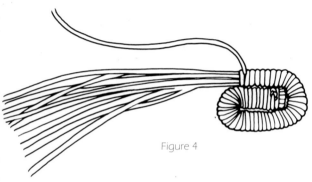

Figure 4

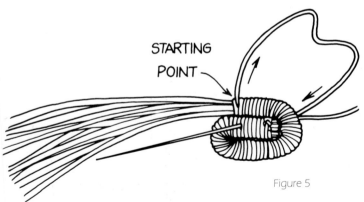

STARTING
POINT

Figure 5

❦ Keeping Coils from Separating

Always catch about one-third of the coil beneath the needles you're stitching in place. If you catch too few needles, they may break under the strain of the thread, and the coils will separate at that spot.

9. The first full stitch, which you're about to take, is called the "starting point." This is a very important location on your basket because you'll make all stitch and shaping changes (and end your basket) on an imaginary line that runs out from it. To take this stitch, bring the sewing needle up and around to the back of the pine needle bundle that rests on the wrapped section. Insert the needle, from the back of your work, through the upper third of the wrapped coil beneath, as shown in Figure 5. (From this point on, you'll always insert the needle from the back of your work and pull it out from the front.)

10. Pass the loose ends of the pine needles through the narrow end of the gauge and out its flared end (see Figure 6).

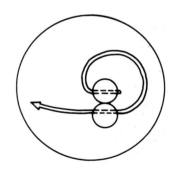

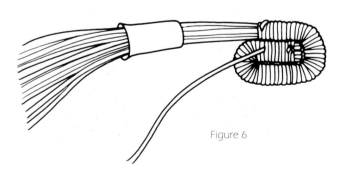

Figure 6

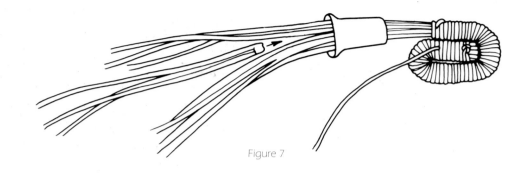

Figure 7

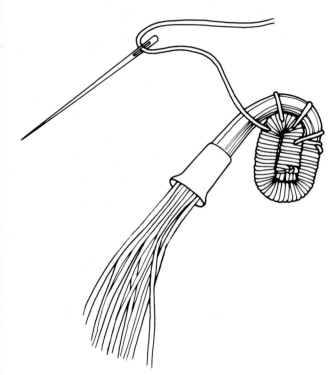

Figure 8

> ### ❦ Preventing Twisted Needles
>
> *The needles that are visible between the gauge opening and your last stitch should always lie flat, with their smooth surfaces facing out. Turning the gauge back and forth a few times or rotating the loose ends of the needles one-quarter turn to the left and right will help straighten them out.*

ADDING NEEDLES

11. Whenever the needles inside the gauge don't hold the gauge snugly in place, you must add needles. (You'll find that you need to do this after every two or three stitches.) Gently spread apart the needles sticking out of the gauge and insert the de-capped ends of two or three single needles—or one cluster—into their center (see Figure 7). Make sure the new needles are centered within the existing bundle, or their whitish heads (once covered by caps) may stick up out of a coil in your finished basket.

STITCHING THE FIRST COIL

12. To make the plain stitch that you'll use for this basket, insert the sewing needle from the back of your work, straight through the top third of the wrapped coil beneath, about 1/8" (3 mm) away from your first stitch. Pull the thread tight, bring your sewing needle up and to the back of your work, and take another stitch, in the same fashion, again about 1/8" away from the last stitch (see Figure 8). Rather than making trial-and-error stabs at a surface you can't see, each time you're about to insert the needle, flip your work over so you can see its back surface.

> ### ❦ Filling the Gauge and Hiding the Needle Ends
>
> *When a gauge is properly filled, it maintains a light grip on the needles inside it and won't slip off. If the gauge is overfilled, you'll have to yank it in order to move it—definitely not desirable! Don't forget to fill the gauge whenever it feels loose.*
>
> *Check the front and back of your basket frequently. If you notice any white needle ends sticking out, use your sewing needle or the point of a scissors blade to push them carefully back into the center of the coil.*

13. Plain-stitch one complete coil by continuing until you've returned to the starting point. Take care to space your stitches evenly; they'll serve as reference points for the stitches in succeeding coils. If they're uneven, the rows of stitches radiating out from your basket's center will be too. Don't forget to add needles as you go.

Stitching Succeeding Coils

14. You may need to add thread at this point. If you do, read Step 16 before proceeding. To take the first stitch of the second coil, insert your sewing needle (from the back of your work) at a slight angle, just to the right of the stitch in the coil beneath and pull it out just to the left of that stitch, picking up about one third of the coil as you do (see Figure 9). Keep the new coil directly on top of the one beneath, or the bottom of your finished basket won't be flat.

15. Continue stitching coils in this fashion, adding de-capped clusters as necessary. Holding the work as shown in the photo above will make the stitching process easier. Because each coil that you add to the bottom of your basket is larger than the one it surrounds, the more you stitch, the farther apart the stitches will be in each coil. In Steps 19 and 20, you'll learn how to add new stitches.

Adding Thread

16. When the thread remaining in your needle is about 4" (10.2 cm) long, remove the needle, leaving the 4"-long tail dangling from the front of your work. Thread another 1-1/2-yard (1.4 m) length into your sewing needle. Take the next

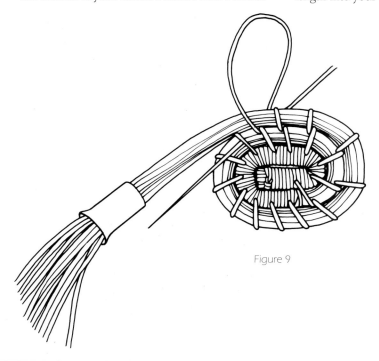

Figure 9

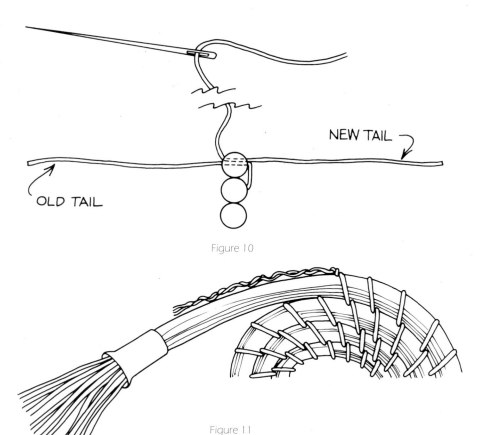

NEW TAIL

OLD TAIL

Figure 10

Figure 11

stitch, but don't pull the thread all the way through the coil. Instead, leave a 4"-long tail at the back of your work (see Figure 10).

17. Using the knot shown in Figure 1 again (see page 15), tie the two short tails together on top of the coil. Then twist the two tails together and fold them over on top of the pine needles to your left (see Figure 11).

18. Take the next plain stitch, which will wrap over the twisted tails and hold them in place. Trim the tails off close to that stitch and continue plain-stitching with your new thread. The knot and tails will be hidden by the next coil.

🌿 Hiding Knots

When you're stitching a coil that will not be covered by another coil and you need to add thread, simply tie the new thread to the old, gauging the position of the knot so that when you take the next stitch, it will be pulled into the center of the coil beneath. Trim the thread ends and tuck them into the coil as well.

ADDING NEW STITCHES

19. When the distance between stitches is approximately 1/2" (1.3 cm), you must add new stitches. First finish a coil by stitching until you've reached the starting point.

20. Now, as you stitch the next coil, double the number of stitches you take (see Figure 12) until you're back at the starting point again. The new stitches will be slanted in appearance. As you begin stitching the next coil, tug each previously-made new stitch gently to the right to help straighten up the stitches on the inside of your basket.

21. Continue to take a stitch over each one in the coil beneath, until the bottom of your basket contains nine complete coils. Stop stitching at the starting point. Press a small piece of masking tape onto the inside bottom of your basket in order to mark the starting point.

complete coil, stopping at the starting point.

23. To make the basket walls flare outward, position each coil so that it rests just slightly to the outside of the one beneath (see Figure 13). As you take each stitch in these coils, gently push the needles outward so that they don't rest directly on top of the coil beneath. Continue in this fashion until you have stitched a total of five coils and have reached the starting point.

FINISHING OFF THE RIM

24. To create an even upper rim for your basket, you must taper the loose pine needles of the sixth (and last) coil in order to blend the end of this coil with the coil beneath. Begin stitching the sixth coil, but stop adding needles when you're about 4" (10.2 cm) from the starting point. Take another stitch or two, but don't add any more needles to the gauge. Hold the basket at eye level to sight across the rim at the starting point and take note of this point at the rim; this is where your last coil must taper flat.

SHAPING THE BASKET WALLS

22. To begin shaping the flared walls of your basket, first bring the next coil up so that it sits right on top of the outermost coil of the basket bottom, as shown in the photo above. Don't try to bring the coil up gradually. Plain-stitch one

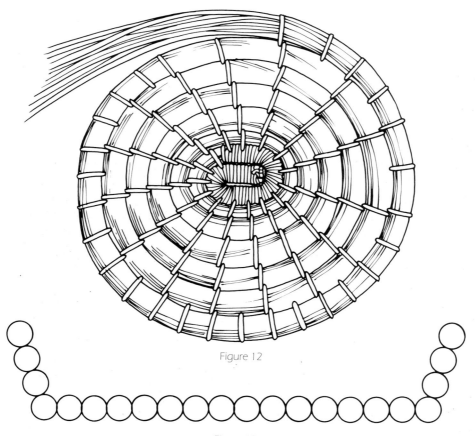

Figure 12

Figure 13

25. Now take a look at the loose needles. If they look too thick to be stitched almost flat at the starting point, remove the gauge and carefully spread apart the loose needles. Then use scissors to snip out one or two needles from the center (and only from the center) of the bundle, as shown in the photo at the top of the next page. Take another stitch or two, sight again, and snip out another needle or two as necessary. Continue stitching and thinning out the needles so that your final stitches cover only a single, flat layer of needles.

26. Take the very last stitch just past the starting point, but don't cut off the thread. You'll now backstitch over the rim in a clockwise direction (see the middle and bottom photos on page 23) to form a series of decorative, X-shaped reinforcing stitches. Take two or three backstitches by inserting the sewing needle into the same holes created when you plain-stitched around this last coil. Bend the remaining loose needles up and back against the first backstitch you took (see Figure 14). Cut the needle ends away at the crease you've just made; then continue backstitching the rest of the rim.

27. To finish off and hide the thread, run your sewing needle into and along a short length of the uppermost coil before snipping off the thread end. Use the point of your sewing needle to tuck the tip of the thread down into the coil.

> ### ❦ Drying and Applying Shellac
> *Before you allow the pine needles to dry or apply any shellac, you may need to hand-mold a damp project into the desired shape and, if necessary, prop it up with heavy objects such as bricks or soup cans. You may even want to use rubber bands or string to help the project retain its shape as it dries. Once a project has been coated with shellac, its shape will be permanent!*

APPLYING SHELLAC (OPTIONAL)

28. Examine the basket closely before it dries. If you see any threads, knots, or whitish pine needle ends, use a pointed object to push them back into the coil. Then allow your basket to dry overnight.

29. Cover your work surface with waxed paper or several layers of newspaper. Place the basket on the paper and, using a small paintbrush, apply a coat of shellac. (The shellac-covered project won't stick to the paper.)

30. When the shellac is completely dry, briskly rub the inside and outside of the basket with a lint-free cloth. This will remove any loose pine needle ends protruding from the coils.

> ### ❦ Using Spray Finishes Safely
> *Make sure you have adequate ventilation when you apply spray acrylic or shellac, and avoid getting any on your skin or clothing.*

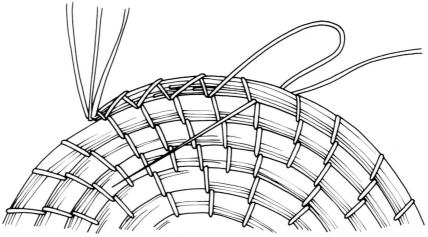

Figure 14

Congratulations! You've just made your first basket. What's more, with the technical skills you've learned in the process, you can make literally hundreds of different baskets, trays, and bowls simply by shaping the coils differently as you stitch them together.

Other variations and embellishments are possible, of course: adding lids and handles, creating basket centers made with materials other than pine needles, using dyed needles or needles with their caps on, and embellishing your baskets with nuts and other small objects. You'll find instructions for these variations in the next two chapters.

CHAPTER THREE

PINE NEEDLE TRANSFORMATIONS

WHAT TRANSFORMS a simple basket into a work of art? Skill, of course, but as you already know, stitching pine needle coils together isn't terribly complex. Creating unique projects is a matter of learning to combine a number of different techniques, from dyeing the pine needles to twisting the coils and adding embellishments. In this chapter, we'll focus on what you can do with the pine needles themselves. In the next chapter, you'll learn new stitches and embellishment techniques.

As you begin to experiment with the variations described in this chapter and the next, remember that no one—not even the world's finest basketmaker—knows better than you what will please you in a finished project. Let your creative energies flow and listen to your imagination. The best pine needle work (and you'll see some displayed in chapter 6) is often the work of artists who allow their imaginations free play.

Browse through these two chapters at your leisure. While they won't teach you everything there is to know about pine needle crafts, they will provide you with all the skills required to move beyond basic basket construction into a world of almost limitless pine needle possibilities.

DYED PINE NEEDLES

Dried pine needles can be dyed almost any color, although to obtain lighter shades, you must begin with needles that have been dried in a dark place. Collect green needles during the first warm months of the year, as they're softer and will accept dyes more readily than mature and harder-surfaced needles. Spread the needles out in a dark location to dry for about four weeks, turning them occasionally to make sure that they color evenly. (If they're exposed to light, they'll turn brown.)

When you're ready to start dyeing, soak no more than 8 ounces (226.8 g) of pine needles in hot water for about ten minutes. Then bring about four quarts (3.785 l) of water to boil in a very large stove-top pot made of enamel or glass. Stir in two packages of powdered household dye (about 2-1/4 ounces or 63.8 g) and

stir until the dye has dissolved. Submerge the pine needles in the dye for about five minutes or until the needles are the desired shade.

To test for color, remove a few needles, rinse them briefly under cold running water, and look at them in the sunlight. When you're satisfied with the shade, remove the rest of the needles from the dye bath, rinse them in cold water, and spread them out on newspapers to dry. When the dyed needles are completely dry, store them just as you would store dry brown needles.

Following are a few extra dyeing tips:

~ To dye only the pine needle caps, stand the needles up in a shallow dye bath, submerging only the caps.

~ While you're set up to dye pine needles, try dyeing gourds, threads, and raffia, too.

~ The liquid dye may be reused but will render less brilliant colors each time.

~ Dyed pine needles that have been dried shouldn't be soaked before using them, as soaking will dilute their colors. Either work with the damp needles right after they've been dyed, or soak only as many needles as necessary to make the center of your basket and used dried, dyed needles in the rest of the basket.

~ There's no way around the fact that the colors will bleed as you work with damp, dyed needles. Wear old clothing and wash your hands frequently if you're using light-colored thread.

To incorporate dyed needles (see page 67), start adding them to the center of the loose needles in the gauge, three or four inches (2.5 or 5.1 cm) before you want the colored needles to appear in the stitched coil. Then, when you reach the point at which you want the dyed needles to show, expose them by snipping off the outer needles in the bundle, close to the last stitch you've taken. Repeat as desired to change coil colors.

PINE NEEDLES WITH CAPS

One way to add texture, depth, and interest to a project is to leave the caps on the pine needle clusters so they'll show on the rim or walls. Use the same basic coiling and stitching technique, but when you add new clusters, position the caps on the top or edge of the bundle instead of burying them within the loose needles. When making small baskets, add clusters one at a time or in groups of two or three. For large baskets, you may add clusters in larger groups.

Because you'll be adding capped clusters at regular, frequent intervals, the coil you create may grow in diameter much faster than a regular coil. You won't use a gauge as you stitch the coil in place, so you must keep an eye on the coil size. Once you've established that size, each time you add a cluster of three needles, remove the same number of needles from the center of the bundle, using sharp scissors to cut

them away at a left-slanted angle. Each time you add three capped clusters, for example, cut away nine needles.

Capped clusters around the upper rim of a project must be placed on top of the coil and must be evenly spaced. Each time you add a cluster (or group of clusters), take a stitch just below the cap (or caps) to hold the new cluster in place. You may add new clusters after each stitch or after every other stitch; just be sure to add them in a consistent fashion. To taper down at the end, trim the needles until only a few remain, take the last stitch, and tuck the few remaining ends under the first group of caps. Backstitch to finish.

ASYMMETRICAL SHAPES

There are two ways to create asymmetrical shapes. One is to widen or narrow the coils in given areas of the project. To widen a coil, use a larger gauge and add more needles than usual as you stitch. To make coils narrower, just use a narrow gauge and add fewer needles. You'll use this technique when you make in-coil handles (see pages 28–30).

Another way to make one section larger than another is to split the coil in two and enlarge each half. To do this, remove the gauge and divide the needles into two sections. Enlarge the lower section by adding more needles, and stitch that section to the coil beneath it, taper-

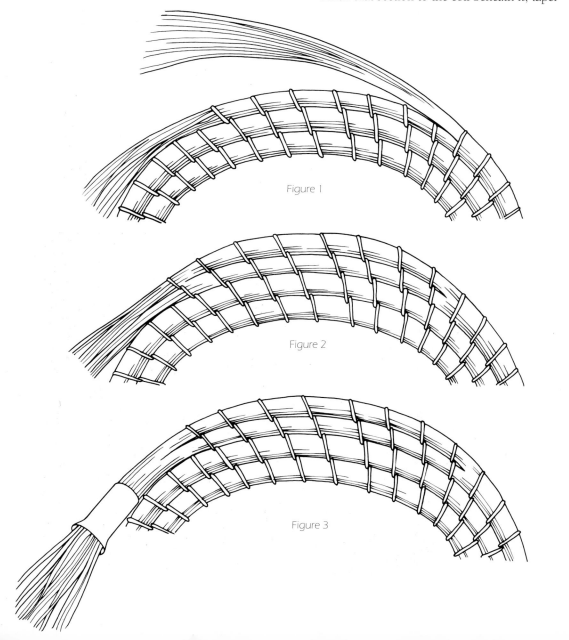

Figure 1

Figure 2

Figure 3

ing off so that only a few needles remain loose at the end (see Figure 1). Then, add needles to the second section and, using a new length of thread, stitch this section to the first section and taper off again, as shown in Figure 2. (To hide the end of the new thread, run the sewing needle up through several coils before taking any stitches.) Finally, fit the loose needles at the ends of both sections back into the gauge and resume stitching a single coil (see Figure 3).

This technique is especially useful when you're making flat lids and find that the outer edges of the lid don't fit exactly into the opening of the basket.

LIDS AND HANDLES

Lids and handles can be made in a number of ways. The photo below shows a flat lid with an in-coil handle, and a dome lid with an add-on handle. One tip before you plunge into the instructions that follow: Making dome lids requires patience and practice. If your first effort yields a less than perfect result, console yourself by remembering that every pine needle basket is a one-of-a-kind creation!

FLAT LIDS

A flat lid, which should be made after your basket is finished, fits snugly into the basket opening, where it rests on a coil ledge just beneath and inside the uppermost rim coil. Because flat lids fit tightly, they must have very secure handles. The pinecone and in-coil handles described in this section are ideal and can be used on dome lids as well.

Flat lids won't fit properly unless the uppermost coils of the basket are vertical, but these vertical coils are easily added to almost any basket. To create the coil ledge upon which the flat lid will sit, first complete all but the uppermost coil of the basket itself. Now stitch the next coil onto the outer edge of the preceding coil. Then stitch the final, tapered coil on top of the outermost coil (see Figure 4) and backstitch to finish.

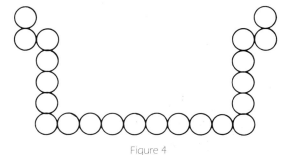

Figure 4

PINECONE HANDLES

Pinecone handles in flat or dome lids actually serve as centers. Start by soaking a pinecone in water until its petals close completely. Knot a length of your selected thread at the base of the cone and wrap the base tightly with several layers of thread. (Thin threads require more layers.) Then knot the thread by inserting the sewing needle under the wrap twice, as shown in Figure 5. The cone will open as it dries, embedding the thread in its petals to make an especially strong handle.

Tie and trim five de-capped clusters as usual. Begin stitching the bundle to the cone as shown in Figure 5. Then continue stitching around the

thread wrap on the cone, treating the wrap as if it were a coil and keeping the stitches 1/4" (6 mm) apart. Continue to shape and stitch the lid around the cone until it is the desired size. Taper off and backstitch as usual. (If your lid is flat, don't worry about ending the coil at the starting point; a correct fit is your primary goal!)

IN-COIL HANDLES

An in-coil handle is simply a continuation of the coil from which the lid or basket is made. To make an in-coil handle for a flat or dome lid, start the lid with any center you like. When the lid is 2" to 4" (5.1 cm to 10.2 cm) in diameter, stop at the starting point and place a small piece of masking tape across the center to help you align the handle correctly. Also make a locking stitch (see page 47) with your thread.

Figure 6 shows how the handle is shaped. Bend the loose needles upward at a 90-degree angle. As you shape the needles to meet the stitched coils on the opposite side of the lid, wind the thread around the needles to simulate 1/4" (6 mm) stitches. Then bend the wrapped needles at 90 degrees where they meet the stitched coils on the other side. The handle will want to lean back; just keep pushing it upright. It will straighten up as you stitch additional coils.

You may notice that the lid now has an extra coil on one side. To accommodate for this fact, make this extra coil as narrow as possible; don't add any needles as you stitch. Then widen the coil opposite to it by adding more needles than usual. Be sure to pull the coils to meet tightly at the handle ends.

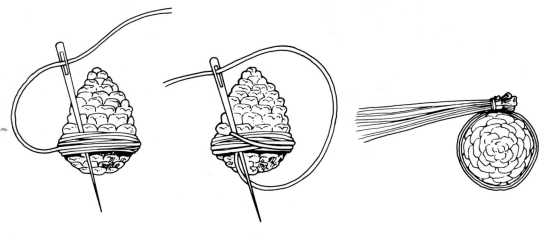

Figure 5

When the coils have evened out, continue stitching until the lid is finished. If you like, you can wrap the in-coil handle with a thin strip of leather. Apply wood glue to the ends of the leather strip and pin them in place until the glue has dried.

To make twisted, in-coil handles for open baskets, first take a look at the innermost basket in the photo to the right. To make this type of handle, stitch only one-half of the last coil on the basket rim. Then bend the needles away from the basket rim, shaping them as shown in Figure 7. As you bend the needles down to meet the uppermost basket coil on the other side, wrap the needles with thread, spacing the

spirals about 1/4" (6 mm) apart. Twist the needles gently as they meet the rim of the basket so that they'll rest on the outer edge of the rim with the loose needles running to the right.

Because the last half-coil of the rim will be running clockwise instead of counterclockwise, it must be stitched in reverse. Hold the basket with the finished portion of the handle close to you and the loose needles at the back of the

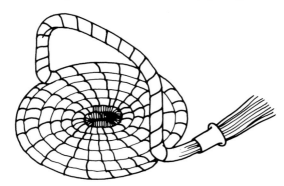

Figure 6

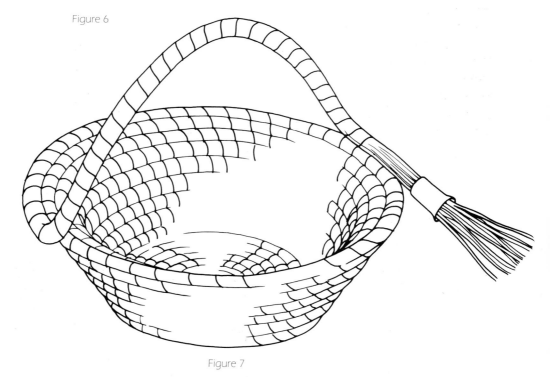

Figure 7

basket, running to the right. To stitch the last half-coil, insert the sewing needle to the left of each stitch on the back (or outside of the basket) so that it will exit to the right of that stitch on the inside of the basket.

Taper off the needles at a point just before the start of the handle. Finish by backstitching over the last half-coil, the handle, and the other half of the rim coil.

In-coil handles for open baskets don't have to stand vertically; they may also extend to the sides to form open handles on the rim of the basket, as shown in the photo on page 57. These handles consist of one or more coils that have been shaped at an angle from the rim of the project. Pull the needles away from the coil beneath and bend them into the desired handle shape, wrapping them with thread as you do. Then bend the needles downward and continue stitching to attach them to the coil beneath.

DOUBLE HANDLES

Take a look at the photo on page 69. This stunning four-coil handle is made in two parts. One two-coil side is constructed as an in-coil handle; the other is started with a new coil. For extra reinforcement, 20-gauge wire is inserted through the first coil on each side.

Stitch the basket until it has the same number of coils on each side. Mark the center with tape. Cut two more pieces of tape, each 2-1/2" (6.4 cm) long; this is the length of the gap between the two sets of handle coils at the base of the handle. Place these two pieces of tape across the rim to mark the locations of the gaps (see Figure 8).

To make the first two-coil handle section, begin by shaping the loose needles on the rim into one handle section, wrapping the handle with thread spaced at 1/4" (6 mm) intervals and adding needles as necessary. Then continue by stitching a second coil next to the first. Taper and finish off the coil at the starting point of the second handle coil (see Figure 9). Now backstitch to cover the last (outer) handle coil and half of the basket rim.

To make the other, two-coil handle section, tie a five-cluster bundle as usual, but trim the needles at the tied end at an angle. Hold the basket

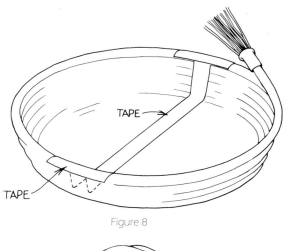

Figure 8

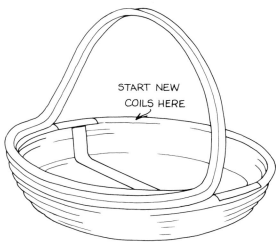

Figure 9

with the finished handle to your left. Attach the tapered end of the new coil to the basket rim, about 2" (5.1 cm) from the right edge of the masking tape, as shown in Figure 9. Stitch this short tapered portion to the rim of the basket, until you reach the edge of the rim tape. Make a locking stitch (see page 47), and then shape the coil to form a two-coil handle as before. Taper and finish off the coil just before the start of this second, two-coil handle section. Backstitch to cover the outer handle coil and last half of the rim.

As a final step, clamp the two handle sections together with clothespins, and stitch the coils together where they touch, hiding the stitches by taking them between coils. If you'd like to add nut slices in the gaps between the two handle sections, at the rim of the basket, simply insert the slices into the gaps and stitch them to the handle and rim coils.

ADD-ON HANDLES

Handles may also be made separately and then stitched to the basket or lid. To make a simple coil handle, tie and trim six to seven clusters together as usual. (For extra reinforcement in long handles, insert a length of 20-gauge wire into the center of the bundle at this stage.) Wrap the desired length with thread, spacing the spirals 1/4" (6 mm) apart and adding needles if necessary. To finish off, wrap the thread around the coil twice, tie a knot, and trim off the needle ends. Sew the handle to the lid, giving it a little twist and/or bending its ends as desired.

The "Little Brown Jug" shown on page 76 has an interesting "zipper" handle, named for the fact that once it's woven, this handle can be shortened or lengthened by pushing the main woven strand up or down.

To make this handle, first tie together three capped clusters and a length of 20-gauge wire, aligning the wire with the central cluster (#3) and knotting the thread just under the caps (see Figure 10). Trim away both thread ends. Cluster #1 will be your primary working cluster.

Begin the weave by bending cluster #1 to the left, over clusters #3 and #2 (see Figure 11).

Next, bring cluster #2 over cluster #1 (see Figure 12).

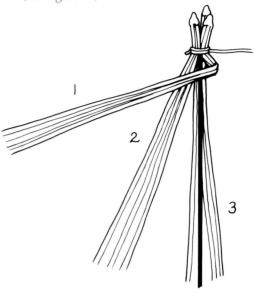

Figure 11

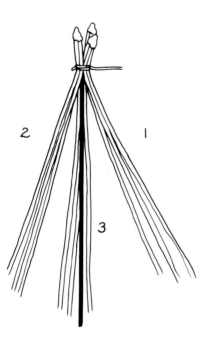

Figure 10

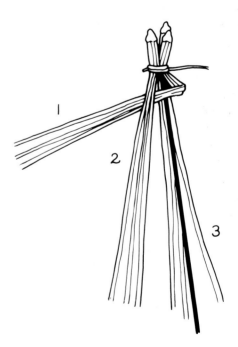

Figure 12

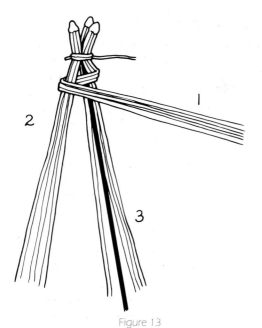

Figure 13

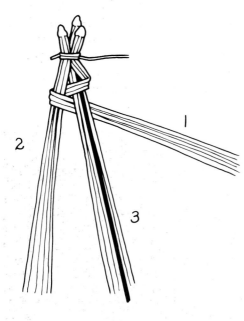

Figure 14

To adjust the length of the handle, either push the primary working cluster (#1) upward to tighten the weave and shorten the handle, or pull cluster #1 down to loosen the weave and lengthen the handle.

To finish off, tie the clusters together and trim away the loose ends. Stitch the handle to your project, shaping it as desired. This handle is not particularly strong, so use it only as a decorative element.

SIT-IN DOME LIDS

To see a good example of a sit-in dome lid, turn to the photo on page 50. Note how the lid nestles into the flared upper coils of the basket rim. To make this lid, use any type of center and handle you like. Stitch and shape the coils as if you were making an upside-down basket.

FITTED DOME LIDS

Fitted dome lids, such as the one shown on page 54, include extra interior coils to hold them snugly in the basket opening. Begin with the center of your choice, incorporating an in-coil handle if you like. Gradually flare the coils outward and downward, always making coil adjustments at the starting point. Gauge your progress by holding the lid over the basket periodically.

When the lid is just large enough to sit on and cover the basket rim, stop stitching without finishing off. You'll now create a series of coils on the inner surface of the lid. These will fit down into the basket opening and will prevent the lid from sliding off the basket (see Figure 15).

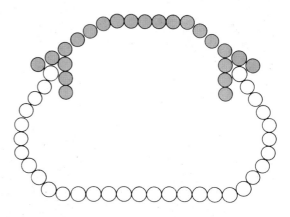

Figure 15

Bend cluster #1 back over clusters #2 and #3 (see Figure 13).

Bring cluster #3 over cluster #1 (see Figure 14).

Continue to shape the handle by repeating the steps shown in Figures 11, 12, 13, and 14: bending #1 over #3 and #2; bringing #2 over #1; bending #1 back across #2 and #3; and bringing #3 over #1.

Start the interior coil by tying and trimming five pine needle clusters as usual. Turn the lid upside down. You'll stitch this coil to the second coil in from the unfinished edge, but in order to keep the stitches from showing through on the outer surface of the lid, either insert the sewing needle between lid coils instead of overlapping them, or use a curved sewing needle.

Stitch another coil onto the interior coil you just stitched in place. Then place the lid on the basket and check to see whether or not the two interior coils extend far enough downward to enter the basket opening. Continue to add coils until the lowest ones fit into the opening snugly. On some lids, two or three interior coils will be sufficient; on others, you may need to add up to six coils. Finish off the interior coils as usual, backstitching for reinforcement. Then return to the rim of the lid and add as many coils as you like. Finish off by backstitching around the rim.

MEANDERING AND TWISTED COILS

A meandering coil is exactly that—a coil that goes wherever you choose to take it. This coil is often a continuation of the coil from which your project is formed, although a separate coil can also be used for this purpose. Meandering coils of either type may also be extended to form footers (see the next page).

Use a curved needle to stitch the meandering coil in place. To secure the thread end and disguise it, run the sewing needle through several coils before trimming the thread and tucking its tip into the coil.

A twisted-coil rim can add a special touch to any coiled basket. First stitch an openwork coil to the rim of the basket in a series of loose-flowing or tight scallops, wrapping the free-standing areas with thread to hold the needles together and stitching the needles to the coil beneath wherever the needles and coil meet. Then shape the next coil to run in and out of the holes in the scallops in the open coil beneath. As you work the twisted coil in and out of the openings, wrap it to simulate stitching.

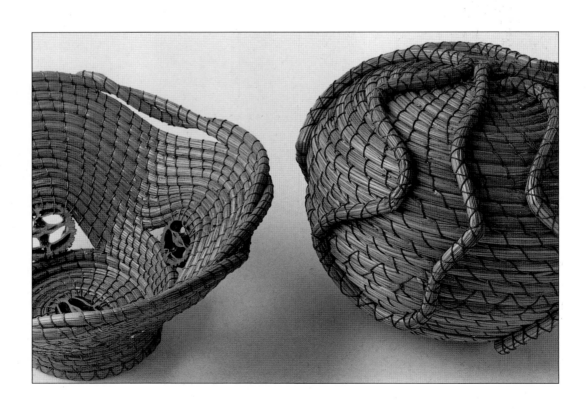

FOOTERS

Footers, which consist of one or more optional coils on the base of a project, protect projects from wear and may also serve as pleasing aesthetic embellishments.

To make a single-coil footer, tie and trim four clusters as usual. Begin stitching the tied bundle to the underside of the outermost bottom coil of your basket. You'll need to start adding needles fairly soon in order to build the coil up to match the size of the basket coils. To finish the footer, you must splice its starting point and the loose needles at the end. As you approach the footer's starting point, spread apart the loose needles at the end of the bundle and blunt-cut a few needles in the center so they'll butt up against the blunt starting point. Nestle the knot at the starting point underneath the remaining needles at the end. Take a few more stitches to bind the remaining needles in place, tapering down as necessary for a smooth finish. Backstitch around the footer to provide extra reinforcement.

Footers may also be shaped from the same coil that makes up the body of the project. The right-hand basket in the photo below is a good example. Yet another variation is the dome footer—a separately constructed, coiled dome

shape that is stitched to the main body of the project (see the photo on page 56).

BRAIDS

Braided pine needles may be sewn to a completed project or coiled and stitched just as you would stitch a plain pine needle coil. Before

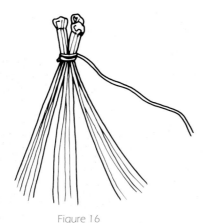

Figure 16

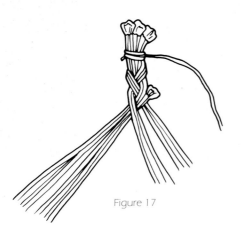

Figure 17

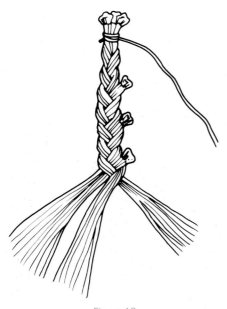

Figure 18

you start, be sure to soak your pine needles long enough to make them flexible.

Tie together three clusters, but leave the caps on (see Figure 16). Also leave the long end of the thread, as you'll need it later. Braid the three clusters twice. Then add a new cluster next to the old one on the left (see Figure 17), with the cap extending about 1/4" (6 mm). (Always add new clusters at the left.) Continue to braid, adding a capped cluster after each two braids, until your braid is as long as desired (see Figure 18). To give you some idea of how long your braid might need to be, turn to "The Little Brown Jug" on page 76. Its coiled braid is more than 8' (2.4 m) in length! Temporarily clamp the end of the braid with a clothespin; you may need to adjust its length later.

To attach the braid to a wood, leather, ceramic, or gourd center (see pages 37–39), first pull it taut to straighten it. Trim off all the short pine needle ends that stick up from the braid. Then cut off the caps at the starting knot and use the length of thread at that end to stitch the braid to the center as if it were a coil, inserting the sewing needle between braid sections. Try to keep the stitching hidden.

To begin an ordinary coil at the end of a braided coil, stop adding pine needles and keep braiding until the loose needles will make up a coil that is roughly the size of the coil you want. Then add the gauge and extra needles if necessary, and continue stitching the ordinary coil.

To finish off a braid, stop adding needles, but continue to braid until the braid itself tapers down. Wrap the thread twice around its end and tie a knot. Trim the needles off below the tie.

CHAPTER FOUR

CENTERS, STITCHES, AND EMBELLISHMENTS

ALTHOUGH COILED NEEDLES will always make up the body of your project, they need not be its primary focus. Delicate and varied stitching, fascinating woven rings implanted within the coils, embellishments such as shells, seeds, and beads, and a wide variety of centers—from wood to leather—can all transform a simple, coiled project into a vehicle for your own artistic visions.

CENTERS

The thread-wrapped center in the pine needle basket you made as you read chapter 2 is only one of many possible basket centers. In this section, you'll learn how to make and use several more.

SOLID PINE NEEDLE CENTERS

These centers are similar to thread-wrapped centers, but the spiraled thread around the starting coil isn't pushed upward to form a solid covering. Instead, the spirals of thread are treated as if they were individual stitches.

Tie and trim three de-capped clusters as usual. Holding the needles upright in your left hand, wind the thread around the pine needles six or

eight times, but don't push the spiraled thread up to the knot. Space the spirals about 1/8" (3 mm) apart to simulate stitches.

Next, carefully coil the wrapped section as shown in Figure 1. Thread your needle and begin stitching the coil, positioning each stitch at a round of the winding thread (see Figure 2). Because you're working with such a narrow coil at this stage, you must insert the sewing needle through the center of the bundle as you stitch. When you've stitched one complete coil, add

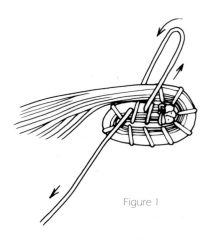

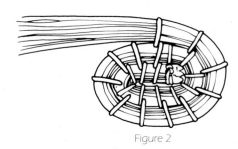

Figure 1

Figure 2

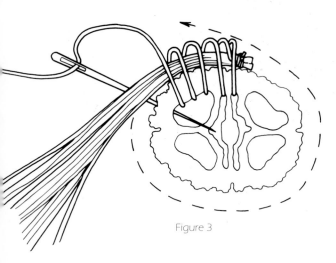

Figure 3

your gauge, expand the coil by adding more needles, and continue stitching the coil as usual.

NUT-SLICE CENTERS

Almost any object with holes around its circumference can serve as an attractive center for a pine needle project. Sliced black walnuts and hickory nuts are fine examples.

To cut rounds that are 1/8" to 1/4" (3 to 6 mm) thick, you can use a coping saw or hacksaw, but a band saw works best. (If you've never used a band saw before, get expert help. These tools can be dangerous!) Clean out the nut meat and any unsightly membrane after slicing and use a toothbrush to scrub out remaining crumbs.

To start a nut center, tie and trim three de-capped clusters as usual. Position the needles along the top edge of the nut, as shown in Figure 3. Thread a sewing needle with the thread extending from the tied cluster and insert the needle, from back to front, through the first small hole in the nut slice. Then, just this once, bring the sewing needle to the back of the bundle and insert it through the bundle's center to anchor the needles to the nut slice.

Next, bring the sewing needle to the back of the bundle again and wrap-stitch to attach the needles around the entire nut slice. In order to space the stitches about 1/8" (6 mm) apart, take three or four wrap-stitches through each large hole in the slice and a single wrap-stitch through each small hole. Space these stitches evenly, as they'll determine the placement of all subsequent stitches.

As you stitch, hold the thread taut to keep the stitched needles tightly in place. When you need to add pine needles, free your hands by using a clothespin to clip the thread and pine needles to the nut. If the needles are long enough to go around the entire nut, wait to add more until you've started the second coil. At this point, your thread will be held by the stitches you've taken.

When you've stitched around to the starting point, hide the knot at the beginning of the pine needle bundle by spreading apart the loose needles to place the knot inside the coil (see

Figure 4). Draw the loose needles over the top of the stitched coil and take one or two stitches to secure the bundle over the knot. Then add your gauge and insert as many pine needles as necessary to fill it. Continue stitching as usual.

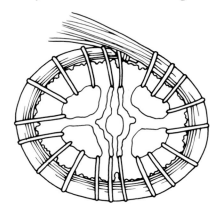

Figure 4

WOOD, LEATHER, POTTERY, AND GOURD CENTERS

Wood centers, 1/4" (6 mm) or less in thickness and in a variety of shapes, also make fine centers. To bore holes around the circumference for your needle and thread, use a 1/16" (1.5 mm) drill bit with a rotary tool, electric drill, or drill press, spacing the holes about 1/4" apart.

Position the tied and trimmed pine needle bundle on the edge of the wood. Insert your needle (from the back) through the first hole in the wood, as shown in Figure 5. Then bring the thread up to overlap the bundle, and—just this once—run the needle through the center of the bundle to hold it so that it won't slide back and forth (see Figure 6). Now wrap-stitch around the center. When you need to add needles, use a clothespin to hold the stitched thread taut and add individual needles rather than clusters, as the single needles will be easier to add to the narrow bundle. Continue as described under nut centers.

Leather, pottery, and gourd centers are all started in the same fashion as wood centers. Rounds of leather are available at leather shops and craft-supply stores, but you can also cut your own 1/8"-thick (3 mm) rounds and pierce holes around their circumferences.

Growing your own gourds is easy. Allow them to mature and dry them thoroughly. Then cut off the top with a fine-toothed saw, jigsaw, or

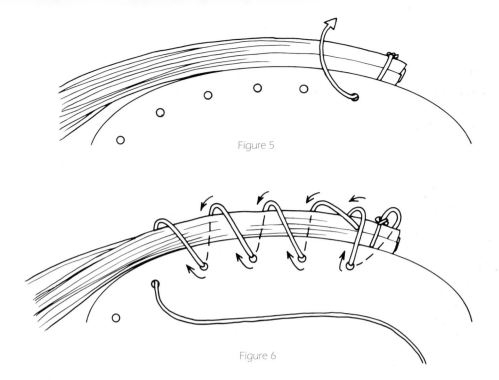

Figure 5

Figure 6

band saw. Clean them out and drill holes around their rims. If gourds aren't a part of your annual garden, purchase them from local gourd growers or gourd societies.

TENERIFFE

The term "teneriffe" refers to a weaving technique in which plastic or metal rings are covered with a woven design. The woven rings are used in pine needle basketry both as basket

centers and as decorative medallions stitched into coils elsewhere in the basket.

First, the ring is covered with double buttonhole stitches to create loops on its inner and outer edges. Then spokes are woven inside the ring to serve as a base upon which to weave the design.

The number of spokes within a ring can vary from six to thirty-six or more, but no matter how many spokes you create, when you weave symmetrical designs, it's easiest to work with a number that is evenly divisible by two different numbers. Why? Let's take a couple of examples.

Twelve is evenly divisible by three and by four. In a twelve-spoke ring, you may weave a design on either three sets of four spokes each or on

four sets of three spokes each (see Figure 7). In a twenty-spoke ring, you can weave on four sets of five spokes or on five sets of four spokes.

Many wonderful teneriffe patterns exist—unfortunately far more than this book can cover, so what you'll find in this section are basic instructions for preparing a twelve-spoke ring and weaving the popular pinwheel pattern. Sketches of some other patterns are provided for those of you who'd like to try your hand at a few variations.

PREPARING THE RING

Plastic and metal rings in many sizes are available at most craft-supply stores. Several sizes work well in pine needle basketry, but a 2"-diameter (5.1 cm) ring is best for beginners.

You'll start by covering the ring with double buttonhole stitches. Cut a 50" (127 cm) length of thread or raffia. (Note that throughout these instructions, we've used the word thread to indicate any stitching material.) Fold the thread in the middle and make a lark's head knot on the outer right of the ring (see Figure 8). Spread the thread ends apart as shown in Figure 9, placing the upper thread (#1) to the right and the lower thread (#2) to the left.

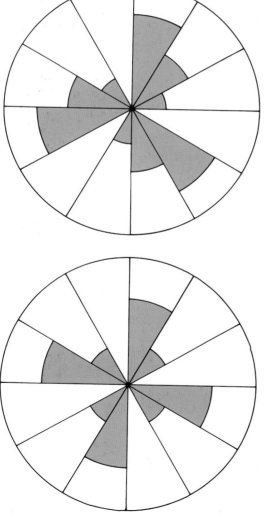

Figure 7

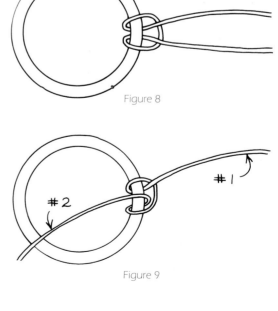

Figure 8

Figure 9

To make the first (single) buttonhole stitch, loop thread #1 over the ring as shown in Figure 10. Then draw the loose end under the ring and up through the loop (see Figure 11). Position this single buttonhole stitch on the outside of the ring.

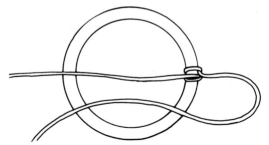

Figure 10

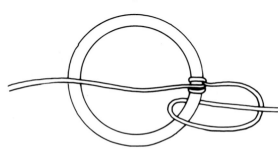

Figure 11

To make the second part of the double buttonhole stitch, form a loop over the ring with thread #2, as shown in Figure 12. Fold the loose thread end under the ring and up through the loop as shown in Figure 13. Position this stitch on the inside of the ring and pull thread #2 back to the left.

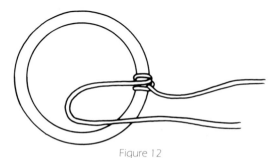

Figure 12

Figure 13

Repeat, working first with thread #1 to make a stitch on the outside of the ring, and then with thread #2 to make a stitch on the inside of the ring. Continue until you have only about 4" (10.2 cm) of thread left and need to add more thread.

Cut a new 50" (127 cm) length of thread and place the middle of it under the ring. Position it parallel and next to the old thread ends. Pull the left end of the new thread up through the ring as shown in Figure 14. Now continue to make alternating knots as before, working each set of two threads together as if it were one. After making a few more buttonhole stitches with the doubled threads, cut the old threads off and continue with the new threads alone.

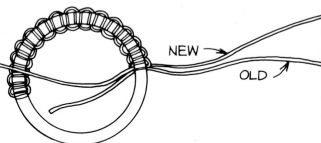

Figure 14

CREATING THE SPOKES

When the entire ring is covered, thread the right-hand thread (#1) into a sewing needle. Finish off this thread by running the sewing needle through a few of the stitches on the outside of the ring (see Figure 15) and trimming off the end close to the last stitch.

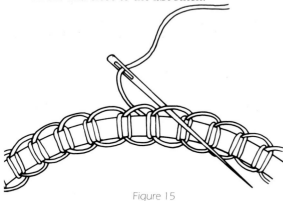

Figure 15

Thread the sewing needle with thread #2. If that thread is at least 20" (50.8 cm) long, you'll use it to start making the spokes, but if it isn't, finish it off by inserting the needle through the stitches on the inside of the ring and trimming off as before. To start a new thread, simply run it through a few of the inner buttonhole stitches to secure it.

To make the 12 spokes, first imagine the ring as the face of a clock and turn it so that your thread and needle emerge at 12 o'clock. Referring to Figure 16, bring the needle down to 6 o'clock and, working from back to front, stitch through the loops on the inside of the ring, until you reach the 7 o'clock position. Now bring the needle up to 1 o'clock and stitch through the loops to 2 o'clock. Come down to 8 o'clock and stitch around to 9 o'clock. Come back up to 3 o'clock and stitch to 4 o'clock. Move up to 10 o'clock and stitch around to 11 o'clock. Move back down to 5 o'clock and bring the thread up to form a double thread from the 5 o'clock position to the center of the ring.

If you have enough thread left to begin weaving, tie a knot in the center of the ring as shown in Figure 17. If your thread is short, finish it off by stitching it into several loops on the outside of the ring and trimming it off. Use a new length of thread to tie the knot in the center. You're now ready to weave a design.

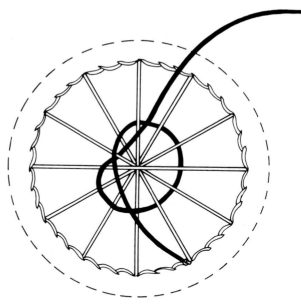

Figure 17

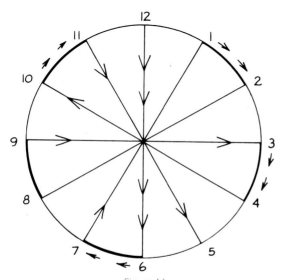

Figure 16

PINWHEEL DESIGN

The pattern shown in Figure 18 is woven on three sets of four spokes each. With the thread extending from the center of the ring, create your first woven row, close to the center knot, by weaving over, under, over, and under the four spokes in one set (see Figure 19). Then turn the ring over and weave the next line on the same four spokes, going under the fourth spoke, over the third, under the second, and over the first. Flip the ring over again and repeat. Continue until the woven rows extend about 1/4" (6 mm) out from the center knot.

Continue the same basic weave on the same set of spokes, but drop the first spoke in that set; weave under, over, and under only the remaining three spokes. Continue weaving around these three spokes until you've woven another 1/4" (6 mm).

Now drop the second spoke as well, so that you're weaving on only two spokes. Weave another 1/4" (6 mm) to complete the pinwheel pattern on this first set of four spokes.

To bring the thread to the next set of four spokes, run the needle down along a spoke within the woven area and out through the center knot, hiding the thread in the woven rows. Repeat the same pinwheel design on the next set of spokes and then on each of the remaining two sets.

When your thread gets short, finish it off by running it down a spoke and into the central knot before cutting it off. Start a new thread by running it up through the knot and back to the point at which you left off.

STITCHING THE PINE NEEDLE COIL TO THE RING

To start your basket with a teneriffe ring, follow the instructions for starting wood centers, but insert your sewing needle through the buttonhole stitches around the ring's outer edge, spacing the stitches about 1/4" (6 mm) apart.

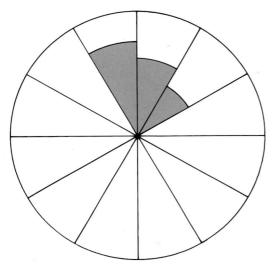

Figure 18

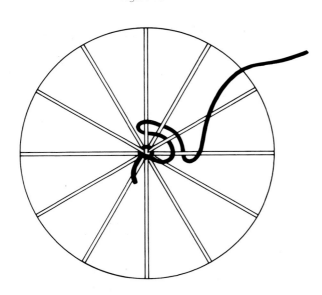

Figure 19

❦ Other Patterns

The pattern illustrations in this section don't come with instructions, but once you've mastered the basic weaving technique, you'll find them easy enough to create. Designing your own patterns is remarkable easy, too. Just sketch in the spoke sections you'd like to cover and then weave to match your pattern.

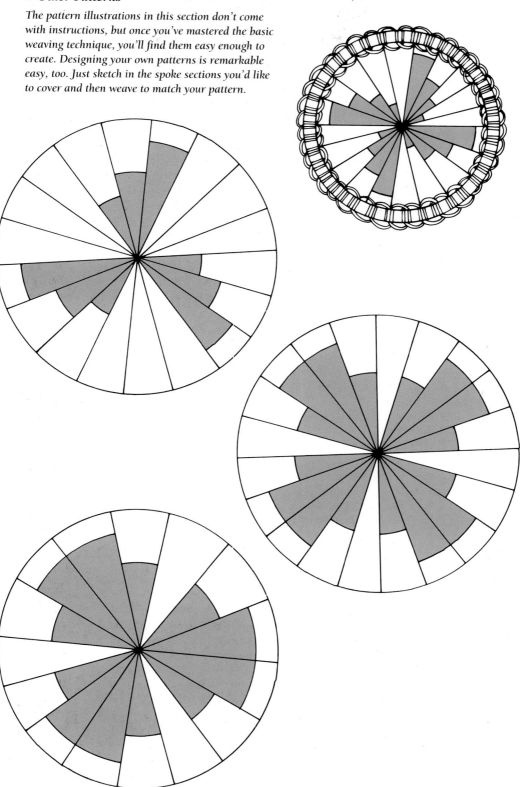

STITCHES

Descriptions of some common decorative stitches follow, but feel free to adapt them or to use others. Keep in mind that unless your basket has a solid pine needle center, you'll need to stitch one complete coil of plain stitches to serve as a base for starting any other type of stitch.

SPLIT STITCH

The split stitch is a variation of the plain stitch which is used with wide threading materials such as raffia. Complete one row of plain stitches first. Then, instead of working your sewing needle from right to left, insert it right through the stitching material in the coil beneath to split the stitch (see Figure 20).

V STITCH

The V stitch may be used with either thick or thin stitching material. Complete your first coil with a plain stitch. If you're using a thick thread such as raffia, as you stitch the next coil, take two stitches through each of the plain stitches in the coil beneath (see Figure 21). The first stitch should split the thread of the stitch beneath, and the second should be taken through the same hole as the first. The V pattern will emerge as you draw your thread to the left to take the next stitch. In subsequent coils, place the V stitches between the legs of the V stitches in the coil beneath.

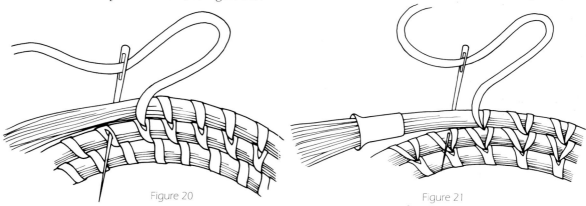

Figure 20   Figure 21

If you're using a thin thread, you obviously can't split the plain stitches in the first coil. Instead, insert the sewing needle so that it exits as close as possible to the plain stitch in the coil beneath. Then take another stitch through the same hole as the first. In subsequent coils, place the V stitches between the legs of those beneath as usual.

WHEAT STITCH

As you can see in Figure 22, the wheat stitch is used with thick threading materials. Start with a coil of plain stitches. Then stitch a row of V stitches, splitting the plain stitches below. In the next and subsequent coils, make the wheat stitches by splitting the first stitch in the coil beneath and then taking a second stitch in the

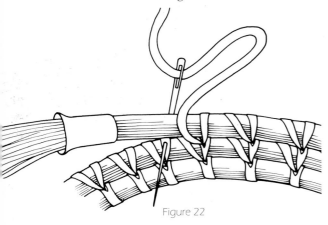

Figure 22

same hole. The wheat stitch you've just created will have one vertical leg (the first stitch) and one leg that leans towards the left (the second stitch). In subsequent coils, the first stitches of each two-part wheat stitch should pierce the vertical leg of the wheat stitch in the coil beneath. (To make a variation of this stitch, split the angled stitch rather than the vertical stitch.)

FERN STITCH

The fern stitch (see Figure 23) is made by first stitching counterclockwise around each coil as usual, with either a V or wheat stitch. On the very last stitch of the coil, take only one lap with your sewing needle to create one leg of the V. Then backstitch over that coil in a clockwise direction, taking one stitch in each previously made hole. These backstitches will create a third leg on each of the stitches in the coil. When you reach the starting point, stitch the next coil counterclockwise with wheat or V stitches again. Reverse again to create fern stitches over the stitched coil. Repeat with each coil.

Among the projects in this book, you'll find a few with fern stitches around their rims. In the charts for these projects, these stitches are identified as backstitches because that's exactly what they are—a single coil of backstitches made over wheat or V stitches.

WRAPPING SECTIONS OF COIL

As the photos on pages 57 and 75 show, one attractive variation to any stitching pattern is to form a solid raffia or thread wrap on one or more sections of coil. If the wrapped section needs to be stitched to the coil beneath, take a stitch, wrap a bit of the coil, take another stitch, and then wrap some more of the coil, repeating the stitch-and-wrap process as desired. If the wrapped section will stand away from the coil beneath, as shown in the photo on page 57, just wrap the coil as you shape it. Bend it down to touch the coil beneath and continue stitching.

ADDED EMBELLISHMENTS

Any object that can be stitched to the exterior of your project or within its coils can serve as an attractive embellishment for your pine needle project.

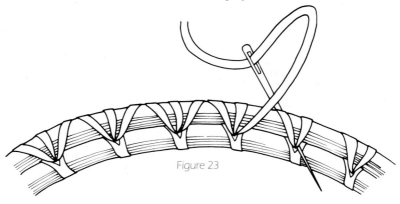

Figure 23

NUT SLICES

To include nut slices, first determine where you'd like to place them in the basket and mark these positions with masking tape. Then shape and stitch the basket as usual until you reach a point about two stitches away from where the nut will be placed. To keep the last stitched thread from slipping loose as you include the nut, you must tighten it down with a locking stitch. Using Figure 24 as a guide, insert the sewing needle from the front of the work to overlap the stitch in the coil. Next, run the needle from the back of the work, through the pine needle coil, to exit at the front of your work, beneath where the nut will be attached (see Figure 25).

Place the nut on top of the coil and stitch through its small holes, as shown in Figure 26. Run the needle back through the coil, from the back of your work, to exit at the front, just to the left of the locking stitch, as shown in Figure 27. (If your sewing needle is too short to do this, run it back through the coil as far as it will go, pull it out from the back of the coil, insert it again, and pull it out from the front, next to the locking stitch.)

To simulate stitches on the needles that rise to meet the nut, wrap the thread around the loose needles. Then wrap-stitch the bundle to the upper edge of the nut. Wrap the other side of the bundle to match the first side and continue stitching the bundle to the coil beneath until you reach the next point at which you want to add a nut.

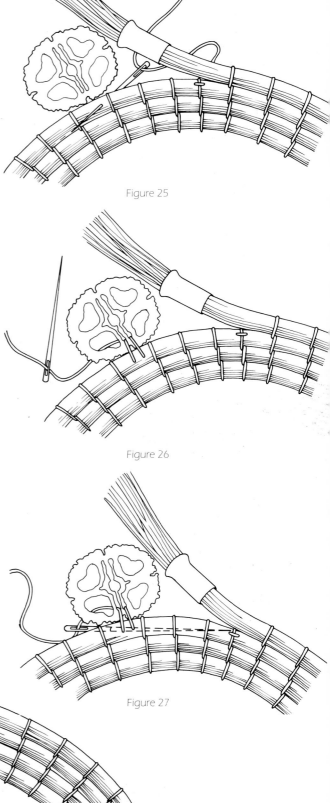

Figure 25

Figure 26

Figure 27

LOCKING STITCH

Figure 24

SEEDS AND BEADS

There are two ways to add small objects with holes in them: thread the needle through the object just before you take a stitch or attach the object to the completed project. To add beads to a finished project, for example, thread the needle through the bead and knot the end of the thread to keep the bead from slipping off. Insert the needle from the outside of the basket and run the thread through the inner coils before snipping it off and burying it. If the basket cups inward at the rim, you may have to stitch the beads into the coils instead.

Job's tears, which have natural holes through their centers, are very attractive embellishments, as are other seeds and small bones.

CHAPTER FIVE

THE PROJECTS

IN CASE YOU WONDER why the projects in this chapter don't include step-by-step instructions, here's the answer: As different as they are from one another, these pine-needle creations are all made by coiling pine needles and stitching them together, a technique you've already learned. What makes each project unique is its combination of the variations described in previous chapters.

Start by selecting a project you'd like to make. Then refer to the chart that comes with it. Every variation included in the project—from the type of thread and stitches used to the embellishments added—is listed in this chart, along with page-number references. If, for example, your selected project has a leather center, braided coils, fern stitches, and a dome lid, the chart will tell you so and will tell you exactly where to look for information on each of these elements. Some projects also include a section called "Special Tips." By all means read these helpful hints; they'll guide you through any special challenges a project may present.

BASIC BASKET VARIATION

JUDY M. MALLOW
2" x 4-1/2" (5.1 x 11.4 cm)

Elements	Page Numbers
Synthetic raffia	10
Thread-wrapped pine needle center	15–17
Split stitch	45

Ginger Jar

Alma P. Hemmings
8" x 7" (20.3 x 17.8 cm)

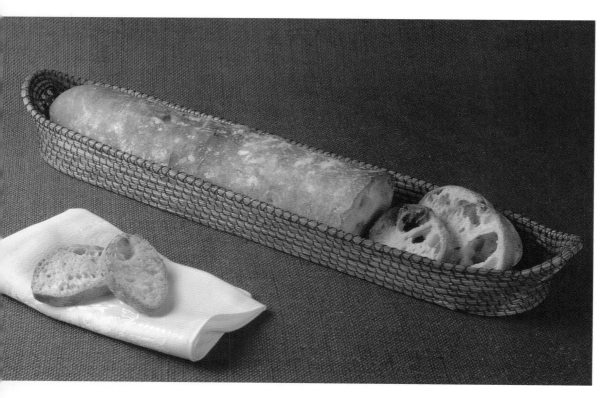

BREAD BASKET

JUDY M. MALLOW
4-1/2" x 22" (11.4 x 55.9 cm)

Elements	Page Numbers
Nylon upholstery thread	10
Wood center	38
Plain stitch	18–19
Backstitch on rim	22
Nut-slice embellishments	47

POTTERY BASE BASKET

JUDY M. MALLOW
5-1/2" x 5-1/2" (14 x 14 cm)

Elements	Page Numbers
Nylon upholstery thread	10
Pottery center	38
Plain stitch	18–19
Twisted coils	33

THREE SKILLETS

VIVIAN P. EVANS
Large: 6-1/2" x 10-1/2" (16.5 x 26.7 cm)
Medium: 5" x 10" (12.7 x 25.4 cm)
Small: 4-3/4" x 8-3/4" (12.1 x 22.2 cm)

ATHENA VASE

CINDY S. HEUER
13" x 10" (33 x 25.4 cm)

Element	Page Numbers
Nylon upholstery thread	10
Solid pine needle center	36–37
Plain stitch	18–19
Backstitch on rim and base	22
Dome footer	34

SPECIAL TIP
Make the vase first. Then add the six-coil footer by starting a new coil at the bottom.

Large Gourd Sewing Basket

Judy M. Mallow
11" x 15" (27.9 x 38.1 cm)

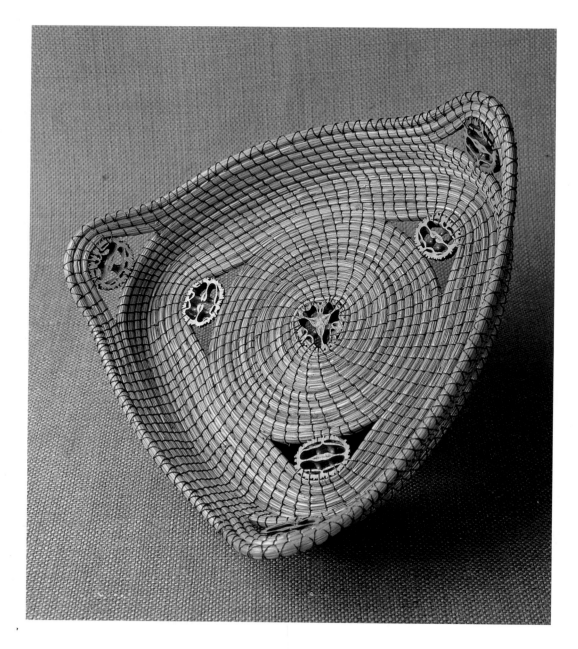

TRIANGULAR BASKET

JUDY M. MALLOW
2" (5.1 cm) high; 12" (30.5 cm) point to point

LARGE OVAL BASKET

NINA P. PRIM

8-1/4" x 12" (21 x 30.5 cm)

Element	Page Numbers
Nylon upholstery thread	10
Solid pine needle center, oval	36–37
Plain stitch (basket bottom)	18–19
Diamond stitch (basket walls)	81
Footer	34
Backstitch on rim	22

SPECIAL TIP
You may make the footer for this piece as an independent coil or as a continuation of the basket coil.

BRANDY SNIFTER

CONNIE P. WILLIAMS

6" x 4-1/2" (15.2 x 11.4 cm)

Elements	Page Numbers
Nylon upholstery thread	10
Solid pine needle center	36–37
Plain stitch	18–19
Backstitch on rim and base	22

SPECIAL TIP
Make the cup section of the snifter first. Then add the stem-and-base section by starting a new coil on the bottom.

SINEW-STITCHED BASKETS

JUDY M. MALLOW

Large: 3" x 10" (7.6 x 25.4 cm)
Medium: 1-3/4" x 7-1/2" (4.4 x 19 cm)
Small: 1" x 5-3/4" (2.5 x 14.6 cm)

THREE-TIERED VASE

CINDY S. HEUER
6-1/2" x 6" (16.5 x 15.2 cm)

Elements	Page Numbers
Nylon upholstery thread	10
Solid pine needle center	36–37
Plain stitch	18–19
Backstitch on rim	22

NAPKIN BASKET

CATHERINE SMITH

5" wide x 9" long (12.7 x 22.9 cm)

Elements	Page Numbers
Raffia	10
Teneriffe center	39–44
Double buttonhole stitch on center handle	40–41
Fern stitch on outer handles and upper coils	46
Wheat stitch	46
Add-on handles (see also "Special Tips")	31–32

SPECIAL TIPS

To make the first of the three handle coils, first tie and trim a five-cluster bundle as usual and insert a 15" (38.1) length of 20-gauge wire into the center of the needles. Then cover the entire 15" length with a double buttonhole stitch, adding pine needles as necessary.

Make another 15" handle section and attach it to the first one, running the stitches through the buttonhole stitches on one side and back-stitching to create a fern stitch. Space the stitches 1/4" (6 mm) apart. Make a third handle section and attach it to the other side of the first section in the same fashion.

Gently bend the three-part handle to shape. Then cut straight across the ends of the coils to trim them. Place the blunt cut ends against the inside bottom of the basket and stitch the coils to the inner walls, making sure that the stitches don't show on the basket exterior.

Use a large rubber band to hold the highest basket sides up as the pine needles dry. The handle ends, which are stitched to the inner surface of the basket, will offer additional support, as will one or two coats of shellac.

CUP AND SAUCER

CONNIE P. WILLIAMS
Cup: 2-1/2" x 4" (6.4 x 10.2 cm)
Saucer: 6" (15.2 cm) diameter

Element	Page Numbers
Nylon upholstery thread	10
Solid pine needle center	36–37
Plain stitch	18–19
Backstitch on rims of saucer and cup and on handle	22
Add-on handle (coil)	31–32
Footer on cup	34

GOURD WITH TAIL

JUDY M. MALLOW
Coiled rim: 4-1/2" x 4" (11.4 x 10.2 cm)

Element	Page Number
Nylon upholstery thread	10
Dipper gourd center	38–39
Plain stitch	18–19
Backstitch on rim	22

Two-Color Swirled Tray

Carolyn C. Register
4" x 12" (10.2 x 30.5 cm)

WOOD-BASE BASKETS

CARL E. LYON
Round: 1-1/2" x 5-1/2" (3.8 x 14 cm)
Oval: 1-1/2" x x 7" (3.8 x 17.8 cm)
Egg: 2" x 6-1/2" (5.1 x 16.5 cm)

Elements	Page Numbers
Raffia	10
Wood centers	38–39
Fern stitch	46

SPECIAL TIPS

The artist who made these baskets used a technique that's not shown in any other project in this book. Before taking each stitch, he twisted the raffia to resemble a thin cord. In addition, rather than piercing the coils with his sewing needle, he inserted the needle between coils, catching the stitches rather than the pine needles to create delicate, lacy baskets with visible spaces between the coils.

STAR BASKET AND
GRADUATED NUT BASKET

JUDY M. MALLOW

Star: 3-1/2" x 8" (8.9 x 20.3)
Graduated Nut: 5" x 9-1/2" (12.7 x 24.1 cm)

FOUR MINIATURES

JUDY M. MALLOW
Pot with lid: 1-1/2" x 1-1/2" (3.8 x 3.8 cm)

Element	Page Number
Nylon upholstery thread or raffia	10
Solid pine needle centers (two oval)	36–37
Plain stitch	18–39
Backstitch (two rims; one handle)	22
One flat lid	27
One in-coil handle	28–30
Seed embellishment (handle on one lid)	48

PENCIL HOLDER

JUDY M. MALLOW
4" x 3-1/4" (10.2 x 8.3 cm)

Element	Page Numbers
Dyed pine needles (dark brown)	24–25
Nylon upholstery thread	10
Solid pine needle center	36–37
Plain stitch	18–19
Backstitch on rim	22

SPECIAL TIPS

Stitch the pine petals to the completed holder one by one, inserting the sewing needle directly through them. Then cut a small pinecone in half lengthwise and stitch it to the project so that it hides the ends of the petals.

TWELVE-NUT TRAY

JUDY M. MALLOW
3" x 15" (7.6 x 38.1 cm)

Two Oval Baskets

Judy M. Mallow
4-1/2" x 9" (11.4 x 22.9 cm)

Elements	Page Numbers
Nylon upholstery thread	10
Solid pine needle centers, oval	36–37
Plain stitch	18–19
Backstitch on rims	22
Nut-slice embellishments	47

SPECIAL TIP
As you can see in the photo, the nut slices are positioned vertically in one basket and horizontally in the other.

DYED NEEDLE BASKET

JUDY M. MALLOW
2-1/4" x 9" (5.7 x 22.9 cm)

Elements	Page Numbers
Nylon upholstery thread	10
Dyed pine needles (red and black)	24–25
Thread-wrapped pine needle center, oval	15–17
Plain stitch	18–19
Backstitch on footer and rim	22
Footer	34

PITCHER

JUDY M. MALLOW
4-1/2" x 3-1/2" (11.4 x 8.9 cm)

Elements	Page Numbers
Nylon upholstery thread	10
Solid pine needle center	36–37
Plain stitch	18–19
Backstitch on footer and rim	22
Dome footer	34
Add-on handle ("zipper")	31–32

SPECIAL TIP
First make the body of this project with one coil.
Then turn the body upside down and make the
dome footer by stitching a new coil to the bottom.

GOURD BASKET

JUDY M. MALLOW
6" x 6" (15.2 x 15.2 cm)

Elements	Page Numbers
Nylon upholstery thread	10
Canteen gourd center	38–39
Plain stitch	18–19
Backstitch on rim	22
Flat lid	27
In-coil handle wrapped with leather	28–30

HESTIA AND FLOW

CINDY S. HEUER
Hestia (right): 3-1/2" x 9" (8.9 x 22.9 cm)
Flow (left): 3-1/4" x 7" (8.3 x 17.8 cm)

Elements	Page Numbers
Nylon upholstery thread	10
Nut-slice centers	37–38
Plain stitch	18–19
Meandering coils and footers	33–34

SPECIAL TIP

The meandering coils and footers on these baskets are formed from the same coils that make up the baskets themselves.

DOUBLE-HANDLED BREAD BASKET

JUDY M. MALLOW

Basket: 4" x 9" (10.2 x 22.9 cm)
Handle: 8" (20.3 cm) high

Element	Page Numbers
Nylon upholstery thread	10
Nut-slice center	37–38
V stitch	45
Backstitch on rim and outer handle coils	22
Double handle	30
Nut-slice embellishments	47

SPECIAL TIPS

Note that the base of each V stitch is located just to the left of the upright leg in the V below.

Stitch the nut slices between the handle sections when the handle is finished.

SMALL POT WITH PINECONE HANDLE

JUDY M. MALLOW
3-3/4" x 4-1/2" (9.5 x 11.4 cm)

Elements	Page Numbers
Artificial sinew	10
Solid pine needle center	36–37
Plain stitch	18–19
Backstitch on rims of basket and lid	22
Flat lid	27
Pinecone handle	28

CERAMIC BASE PLANT HOLDER

JUDY M. MALLOW
5" x 6" (12.7 x 15.2 cm)

Element	Page Numbers
Nylon upholstery thread	10
Ceramic center	38
Plain stitch	18–19
Nut-slice embellishments	47
Twisted coil	33

SPECIAL TIP
Note that the twisted coil runs through not one, but two coils on the rim.

GOURD BASKET

JUDY M. MALLOW
8" x 10" (20.3 x 25.4 cm)

THREE-NUT TRAYS

JUDY M. MALLOW
Large: 3-1/2" x 10" (8.9 x 25.4 cm)
Medium: 3-1/2" x 8" (8.9 x 20.3 cm)

GOURD BASKET WITH DOME LID

JUDY M. MALLOW
8-1/2" x 7-1/2" (21.6 x 19.1 cm)

Element Page Numbers

Nylon upholstery thread   10

Birdhouse gourd center   38–39

Plain stitch   18–19

Backstitch on rims of basket and lid   22

Sit-in dome lid   32

In-coil handle   28–30

THREE GOURDS
(DYED, STAINED, AND NATURAL)

JUDY M. MALLOW

Large: 7" (17.8 cm) high; brown stain
Medium: 4-1/2" (11.4 cm) high; natural
Small: 4-1/2" (11.4 cm) high; purple dye

Elements		Page Numbers
All:	pine needles with caps	25–26
	gourd centers	38–39
	plain stitch	18–19
Large:	nylon upholstery thread	10
Medium:	nylon upholstery thread	10
Small:	artificial sinew	10

WRAPPED COIL BASKET

CAROLYN C. REGISTER

2" x 9" (5.1 x 22.9 cm)

SMALL BASKETS

JUDY M. MALLOW

Large: 2" x 5-1/2" (5.1 x 14 cm)
Medium: 1-3/4" x 4" (4.4 x 10.2 cm)
Small: 1" x 2" (2.5 x 5.1 cm)

Element	Page Numbers
Nylon upholstery thread	10
Nut-slice centers	37–38
Plain stitch	18–19
Backstitch on rims and handles	22
In-coil handles	28–30

LITTLE BROWN JUG

JUDY M. MALLOW

5-3/4" x 4-1/2" (14.6 x 11.4 cm)

Element	Page Numbers
Nylon upholstery thread	10
Wood center	38
Plain stitch	18–19
Backstitch on rim	22
Braids	34–35
Add-on handle ("zipper")	31–32

SPECIAL TIPS

Start by making an 8'-long (2.4 cm) braid.
Stitch the braid to the wood center with the
caps on the outer surface. When you reach the
point at which you want to blend the braid into
a coil, refer to page 35 for instructions.

You'll need to use a curved sewing needle as
you stitch the tight, curved neck of the jug.

HESTIA STRAIGHT-SIDED BASKET

CINDY S. HEUER
3-1/2" x 9" (8.9 x 22.9 cm)

SPECIAL TIP

Although it's not visible in the photo, this basket has a meandering coil that extends from the rim downward to become a footer on the bottom.

DYED GOURDS

JUDY M. MALLOW
Large: 4" x 2" (10.2 x 5.1 cm)
Small: 2-1/4" x 3" (5.7 x 7.6 cm)

PIN-CUSHION SEWING BASKET

JUDY M. MALLOW
2" x 6-1/2" (5.1 x 16.5 cm)

SPECIAL TIPS

First make the large basket. To add the center section, start stitching a new coil inside the basket, building it to four coils in height.

The pin cushion shown in the photo was made by covering steel wool with burlap.

Gourd Sewing Basket

Judy M. Mallow
7-1/2" x 12" (19.1 x 30.4 cm)

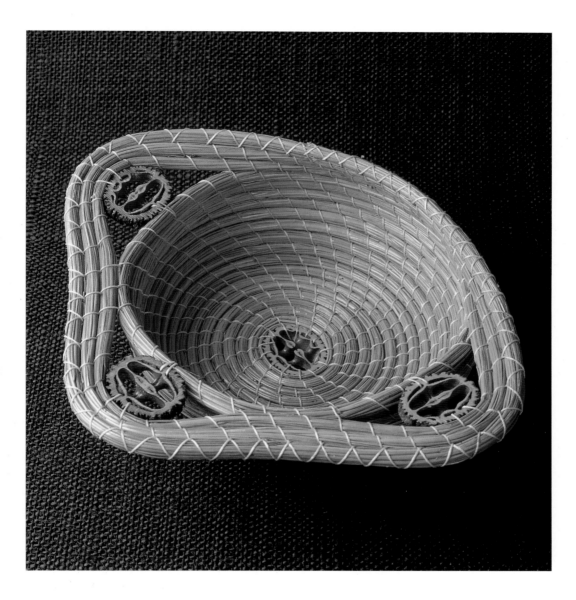

THREE TOES

CINDY S. HEUER
3-1/2" x 10" (8.9 x 25.4 cm)

Elements	Page Numbers
Nylon upholstery thread	10
Nut-slice center	37–38
Plain stitch	18–19
Backstitch on rim	22
Nut-slice embellishments	47

DIAMOND-STITCH BASKET

NINA P. PRIM

4" x 9-1/2" (10.2 x 24.1 cm)

Element	Page Numbers
Nylon upholstery thread	10
Solid pine needle center	36–37
Plain stitch (basket bottom)	18–19
Diamond stitch (basket walls)	below
Footer	34

SPECIAL TIPS

The diamond stitch used in this project has the most pleasing visual effect when it appears on the walls of a basket rather than on the basket floor. Start by plainstitching all the floor coils.

First coil: Pull the needles upward to start shaping the basket walls and plain stitch one complete coil. Then backstitch around this coil.

Second coil: Plain-stitch the second wall coil, following the plain stitches (not the backstitches) in the coil beneath. This will create the bottom halves of the stitched diamonds. Now back-stitch around the coil, inserting the needle through the plain-stitch holes, but instead of pulling the sewing needle out to the left of the stitch in front, pull it out straight toward you, to the right of the stitch.

Third coil: Plain-stitch this coil, but instead of following the plain-stitch in the second coil, insert the sewing needle from the back to exit directly under the cross formed by the back-stitch on the second coil. You won't be able to see the crossed threads, of course, as they'll be hidden by the loose needles, but the legs of the upside-down V can serve as your guides. Now backstitch through the same holes made when you plainstitched this coil.

Fourth and subsequent coils: To continue, just repeat the stitches you made on the third coil.

The footer on this basket is made with an independent coil.

SPHERE WITH MEANDERING COILS

CINDY S. HEUER
6" x 7-1/2" (15.2 x 19.1 cm)

Elements	Page Numbers
Nylon upholstery thread	10
Nut-slice center	37–38
Plain stitch	18–19
Backstitch on meandering and center coils	22
Meandering coil	33

SPECIAL TIPS

This project is made with a single, continuous coil. As you complete the sphere, you must use a curved needle to stitch the closing coils, as the back of your work will be hidden within the sphere.

As soon as you've stitched the sphere closed, pull the coil to the outer surface to form the meandering coil and stitch it in place with a curved sewing needle.

CHAPTER SIX
A GALLERY

THE OLD ADAGE, "practice makes perfect," is true, of course, but fine basketmakers bring more than patience and well-developed technical skills to their work. Outstanding basketmakers are those who understand that even the humblest of materials, when approached with love and respect, lend themselves to an endless array of forms and expressions.

As well as being excellent examples of fine technique, the works shown in this chapter give testimony to the warmth, simplicity, and timelessness of pine needles themselves. Whether the needles appear in elegant, tall baskets, mysterious masks, colorful sculptures, or trays, they lend an elemental sense of the earth itself to everything made with them.

SILENT BEAUTY

LEE SIPE
Length and width: 29" x 21" (73.7 x 53.3 cm)
1984

COLOR-GO-ROUND

JUDY M. MALLOW
Height and diameter: 4-1/2" x 10" (11.4 x 25.4 cm)
1995

UNTITLED

ETHEL S. CLIFFORD
Height and diameter: 3" x 8-1/2" (7.6 x 21.6 cm)
1995

BELLE CHER

JUDY M. MALLOW
Height and length: 3" x 9" (7.6 x 22.9 cm)
1991

FRINGES OF DARKNESS

JUDY M. MALLOW

Height and diameter: 7" x 5" (17.8 x 12.7 cm)

1991

GRECIAN URN

LEE SIPE
Height and diameter: 27" x 15" (68.6 x 38.1 cm)
1986

ENDLESS NEEDLE

LEE SIPE
Height and diameter: 34" x 11" (86.4 x 27.9 cm)
1991

Untitled

Ethel S. Clifford
Height and diameter: 4" x 9" (10.2 x 22.9 cm)
1996

UNTITLED

ETHEL S. CLIFFORD
Height and diameter: 4" x 7" (10.2 x 17.8 cm)
1996

SERVING TRAY

JUDY M. MALLOW

Height and length: 3" x 20" (7.6 x 50.8 cm)
1994

EASTER SURPRISE

LEE SIPE

Length and height: 21" x 19" (53.3 x 48.3 cm)

1985

Not a Hat

Judy M. Mallow

Height and width: 4" x 7" (10.2 x 17.8 cm)
1991

MIDNIGHT CHALICE

JUDY M. MALLOW

Height and diameter: 7" x 5" (17.8 x 12.7 cm)
1990

BIG MOUTH

JUDY M. MALLOW

Height and length: 5" x 7-1/2" (12.7 x 17.8 cm)
1991

MYSTERY

LEE SIPE

Depth and diameter: 6" x 31" (15.2 x 78.7 cm)

1985

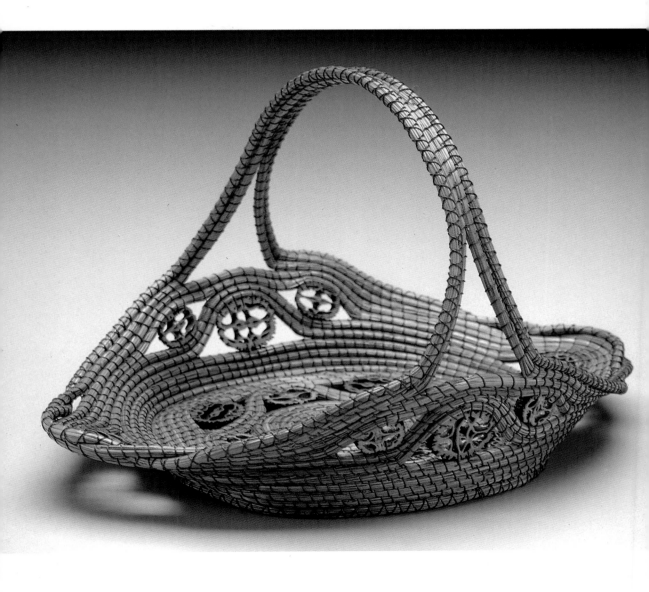

THE ROSE GARDEN

JUDY M. MALLOW

Height and length: 11" x 16" (27.9 x 40.6 cm)

1996

RED FACED MASK

JUDY M. MALLOW
Width and length: 8" x 13" (20.3 x 33 cm)
1992

ARDENT PROWESS

LEE SIPE
Height and diameter: 31" x 20" (78.7 x 50.8 cm)
1987

MENDED WAVE

LEE SIPE

Height and diameter: 15" x 19" (38.1 x 48.3 cm)
1995

THE FAT LADY SINGS

JUDY M. MALLOW
Height and width: 6-1/2" x 10" (16.5 x 25.4 cm)
1990

POT OF GOLD

JUDY M. MALLOW

Height and diameter: 6-1/2" x 8" (16.5 x 20.3 cm)
1993

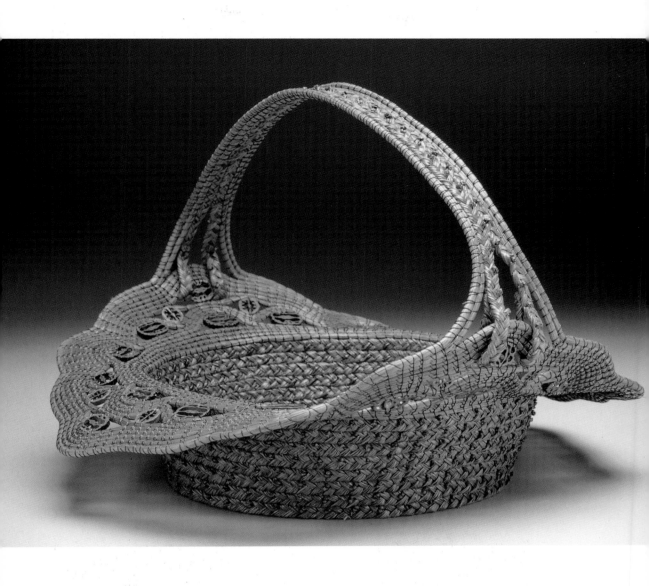

Ultima

Judy M. Mallow

Height and length: 17" x 26" (43.2 x 66 cm)
1989

CHAPTER SEVEN

HISTORY

PINE NEEDLE CRAFTING has probably existed for as long—and in as many places—as people and pine trees have shared the earth. While pine trees aren't indigenous to every country in the world, they do grow widely and today can be found in North and Central America, South Africa, the Canary Islands, Mexico, Australia, New Zealand, and from the Philippines to Burma and northern China. Because the threading material used in the earliest pine needle baskets disintegrated, however, and because written records of the history of this craft are so sparse, the origins of pine needle basketry may always remain shrouded in mystery.

We do know that the tradition of stitching grass coils together to make baskets and other items is centuries old. In western and central Africa, gifted artisans perfected the coiling technique, and their skills traveled with them when they were brought to North America as slaves. Today, some of the finest specimens of coiled basketry in the United States are made by the descendants of these slaves—the Gullah Afro-Americans of coastal South Carolina. Their exquisite coiled baskets are usually made with grasses, which unfortunately are less abundant every year, but many Gullah basketmakers also incorporate pine needles into their work.

Braided basket with split and twisted coil handle

Artist unknown

Pine needle baskets sewn with flat reed. Benguet pine needles indicate that these baskets may have been made in the Philippines.

Sweet grass basket with contrasting pine needle band at bottom and on lid

Artist unknown

Double-handled basket made during the 1950s by the author's grandmother, Nina Prim

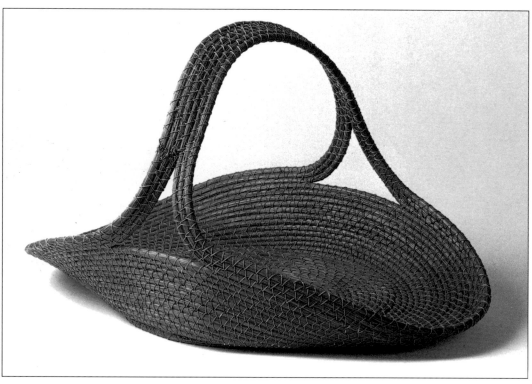

Both the Seminoles of Florida and the Coushatta (or Kousati)—a tribe originally from Alabama, which dispersed to Georgia, Louisiana, and Florida—use pine needles in their basketry. Swamp-cane was the material of choice for these Native Americans, but as increased cultivation of land destroyed their cane sources, they turned increasingly to pine needles as their primary material.

When were pine needles were first used in coiled baskets? We may never know. In 1917, a North Carolina Superintendent of Schools, William Hammel, credited Mrs. M. J. McAfee, of West Point, Georgia, with making the first coiled pine needle project. Mr. Hammel explained that Mrs. McAfee, in an effort to supply hats for her family during the Civil War, invented the technique of coiling pine needles and successfully made a pine needle hat for her grandfather.

Mrs. McAfee, who became an extremely skilled pine needle basketmaker and teacher, may have witnessed the coiling technique used by slaves in her state, and she may have been aware of the pine needle basketry tradition of Native Americans in her area. In any event, by the turn of the century, coiled pine needle work was appearing in states as far away as Illinois, and in 1917, *The Ladies Home Journal* advertised an instructional pamphlet for readers interested in making pine needle baskets. As the decades passed, pine needle crafting was even recommended as a recreational handcraft for young women in school and for women's groups. When the Bureau of Indian Affairs introduced economics programs to encourage Native Americans to produce marketable handcrafts, pine needle basketry was one of the handcrafts taught. Several Native American tribes now produce stunning pine needle baskets.

Perhaps because pine trees grow only in certain areas, pine needle basketry has not been quite as popular as other basketry techniques. In recent years, however, a renewed interest in traditional crafts has brought increasing attention from professional basketmakers and hobbyists alike. Today, it's not uncommon to see contemporary pine needle baskets in fine galleries, alongside baskets made by the artists' mothers and grandmothers.

V-stitched basket with braided handle, found in Boone, North Carolina

Artist unknown

ACKNOWLEDGEMENTS

Pine Needle Basketry could not have been written without the support and encouragement of the contributing designers listed on this page. I'm very grateful to them all.

Ethel Skeans Clifford (pages 48, 85, 90, and 91), of Deer Isle, Maine, worked for 20 years at the Haystack Mountain School of Crafts and has been attending basket workshops since 1986. Her work is represented by the Blue Heron Gallery in Deer Isle and by Island Artisans, in Bar Harbor, Maine.

Vivian Prim Evans (page 52), of Carthage, NC, has retired from the work world but not from pine needle basketry. She has won several blue ribbons in local and state competitions held by the Homemakers Club.

Alma P. Hemmings (page 50) was the sister of the author's grandmother and an exceptional pine needle basketmaker as well as painter. She was well known and loved in the North Carolina mountains where she lived and died.

Cynthia Shoffner Heuer (pages 5, 33 right, 34 bottom right, 53, 58, 68 bottom, 77, 80, and 82) lives in Pittsboro, NC. She is an ardent pine needle basketmaker whose designs are innovative and challenging. Her baskets are in the homes of many collectors.

Carl E. Lyon (page 62) lives in Traverse City, Michigan. Carl learned to work with pine needles the hard way, he says, "through trial and error, more than 30 years ago." At the young age of 96, Carl is still making his distinctive baskets.

Carolyn Crouse Register (pages 39, 61, and 75), of Pinehurst, NC, has retired from the North Carolina Cooperative Extension Service but still volunteers as a teacher of pine needle basketry through the Moore County Home Extension Homemakers Association.

Lee Sipe (pages 83, 88, 89, 93, 97, 100, and 101), a native of Masan, Korea, now resides in Columbia, South Carolina. She explains that her oriental heritage has helped her "to appreciate the unusual beauty in the common, the simple, and the ordinary as well as the beauty of form and detail." Ms. Sipe, who uses natural dyes and who creates her own pottery bases for some baskets, has won several awards for her work.

Catherine Smith (page 59), who died several years ago, was a respected basketmaker and appeared annually at the North Carolina State Fair as a member of the "Village of Yesteryear." Some of her baskets are part of the permanent collection at the Smithsonian, and she was invited to participate in one World's Fair.

Connie Prim Williams (pages 12, 56 bottom, and 60 top), the author's mother, is a fourth-generation (and very active) basketmaker from Carthage, NC, who has demonstrated her craft at the North Carolina State Fair for many years. Connie contributes greatly to this craft by gathering pine needles for grateful daughter!

Thanks, too, to the wonderful people at Lark Books (Asheville, NC): publisher *Rob Pulleyn*, for his role in keeping our heritage crafts alive for all to share; *Chris Rich*, my editor, for making my writing possible and pleasurable; art director *Kathy Holmes*, for her vision and hard work; and *Evan Bracken* (Light Reflections, Hendersonville, NC), the photographer contracted by Lark to take most of the fine photos in this book.

Special thanks go to *Andrew Glasgow*, *Wendy Outland*, *Carol Carr*, and *Nona Donoho* at the Blue Spiral gallery in Asheville, NC, for permitting Evan to photograph the baskets of Lee Sipe; to *Jane Przybysz*, Principal Investigator, Southeastern Crafts Revival Project, McKissick Museum, University of South Carolina, for her remarkable generosity in helping me locate historical information; to *Tim Barnwell* (Asheville, NC), who took the photos on pages 86, 87, 94, 98, and 104; and to *McKenzie and Dickerson* (Southern Pines, NC) for the photo on page 7.

Last but not least, my heartfelt thanks to three special women; my mother, *Connie Prim Williams,* who encouraged me from the beginning to follow my heritage and my heart; my best friend, *Cindy Heuer*, whose support through the years has helped me keep doing what I love doing best—making pine needle baskets; and my grandmother *Nina Poindexter Prim* (pages 56 top, 81, and 106), my mentor and teacher during her lifetime and now a guardian angel in mine—love forever.

PINE SPECIES AND NEEDLES

Although pine needles are available from suppliers, you may very well want to gather your own. Few activities can be as rewarding. A chart of suitable pine species and their average needle lengths follows:

Name	Alternate Name	Botanical Name	Location	Needle Length
Benguet Pine		*Pinus insularis*	Philippines north to Burma and southern China	9" (22.9 cm)
Canary Islands Pine		*Pinus canariensis*	Canary Islands. Although not indigenous, also found in southern California	9" to 12" (22.9 to 30.5 cm)
Chir Pine		*Pinus roxburghii*	Himalayas. Although not indigenous, also found in California	8" to 12" (20.3 to 30.5 cm)
Coulter Pine	Big Cone Pine	*Pinus coulteri*	Western North America	10" (25.4 cm)
Digger Pine	Nut Pine; Gray Pine	*Pinus sabiniana*	Western North America	8" to 12" (20.3 to 30.5 cm)
Guatemala Pine		*Pinus pseudostrobus*	Mexico and Central America	16" (40.6 cm)
Jeffrey Pine	Western Yellow Pine; Bull Pine	*Pinus jeffreyi*	Western North America	5" to 10" (12.7 to 25.4 cm)
Loblolly Pine	Oldfield Pine; North Carolina Pine	*Pinus taeda*	North America; New Jersey south to Florida, west to Texas and north to Oklahoma	5" to 9" (12.7 to 22.9 cm)
Longleaf Pine	Longleaf Yellow Pine; Georgia Pine; Southern Yellow Pine; Yellow Pine	*Pinus palustris*	North America; coastal plain from southern Virginia to Florida; west to Texas	10" to 18" (25.4 to 45.7 cm)
Montezuma Pine	Mexican Pine	*Pinus montezumae*	Mexico to Guatemala; southern California	15" (38.1 cm)
Pond Pine	Marsh Pine; Pocosin Pine	*Pinus serotina*	North America; New Jersey and Delaware south to Florida	5" to 8" (12.7 to 20.3 cm)
Ponderosa Pine	Western Yellow Pine; Silver Pine	*Pinus ponderosa*	North America; Southern British Columbia to Mexico and east to South Dakota and Nebraska	5" to 10" (12.7 to 25.4 cm)
Red Pine	Norway Pine	*Pinus resinosa*	North America; Manitoba east to Nova Scotia and south to Pennsylvania. Although not indigenous, also found in Australia, New Zealand, and South Africa	4" to 6-1/2" (10.2 to 16.5 cm)
Slash Pine	Yellow Slash Pine; Swamp Pine	*Pinus elliottii*	Location: Eastern North America; South Carolina to Florida and west to Louisiana. Although not indigenous, also found in Australia, New Zealand, and South Africa	7" to 10" (17.8 to 25.4 cm)
Telecote Pine	Mexican Yellow Pine	*Pinus patula*	Mexico	up to 12" (30.5 cm)
Torrey Pine	Del Mar Pine; Soledad Pine	*Pinus torreyana*	Natural habitat is Torrey Pine Preserve, a small area north of San Diego and on Santa Rosa Island	13" (33 cm)

METRIC CONVERSION CHARTS

INCHES	CM		INCHES	CM		VOLUMES	
1/8	0.3		20	50.8		1 fluid ounce	29.6 ml
1/4	0.6		21	53.3		1 pint	473 ml
3/8	1.0		22	55.9		1 quart	946 ml
1/2	1.3		23	58.4		1 gallon	3.785 l
5/8	1.6		24	61.0		(128 fl. oz.)	
3/4	1.9		25	63.5			
7/8	2.2		26	66.0		**WEIGHTS**	
1	2.5		27	68.6		0.035 ounces	1 gram
1-1/4	3.2		28	71.1		1 ounce	28.35 grams
1-1/2	3.8		29	73.7		1 pound	453.6 grams
1-3/4	4.4		30	76.2			
2	5.1		31	78.7			
2-1/2	6.4		32	81.3			
3	7.6		33	83.8			
3-1/2	8.9		34	86.4			
4	10.2		35	88.9			
4-1/2	11.4		36	91.4			
5	12.7		37	94.0			
6	15.2		38	96.5			
7	17.8		39	99.1			
8	20.3		40	101.6			
9	22.9		41	104.1			
10	25.4		42	106.7			
11	27.9		43	109.2			
12	30.5		44	111.8			
13	33.0		45	114.3			
14	35.6		46	116.8			
15	38.1		47	119.4			
16	40.6		48	121.9			
17	43.2		49	124.5			
18	45.7		50	127.0			
19	48.3						

BIBLIOGRAPHY

Armstrong, Katherine L. *Fragrant Basketry: The Pine Needle and Raffia Handbook.* Robson, BC: Bear Grass Press, 1986.

Hammel, William, C.A. *Pine-Needle Basketry in Schools.* Seattle: The Shorey Bookstore, 1972.

James, George W. *Practical Basket Making.* Seattle: Shorey Book Store, 1966.

Land, Marie. *The Art of Pine Needle Basketry.* Lilburn, GA: Corner Cupboard Crafts, 1978.

Lang, Minnie McAfee. *Basketry Weaving and Design.* New York: Charles Scribner's Son, 1925.

McFarland, Jeannie. *Advanced Pattern Book for Pine Needle Raffia Basketry.* Redmond, Oregon: Midstate Printing, 1980.

Millikin, Linna L. *Pine Needle Basketry: A Complete Book of Instructions for Making Pine Needle Baskets.* Cambridge: J.L. Hammett, 1920.

Mallow, Judy Mofield. *Pine Needle and Nut Crafting.* Raleigh, NC: Glover Printing, 1984.

Mulford, Judy. *Basic Pine Needle Basketry.* [Los Angeles: Judy Mulford], 1986.

Walsh, Veronica T. *The Book of Pine Needle Craft Instruction.* Seffner, FL: Do Do Sales, 1977.

INDEX

Pine Needle Basketry